Mongol Empire

The Man Behind the Mongol Empire

(The History and Legacy of the Mongol Empire's Capital)

Janet Corbett

Published By **Chris David**

Janet Corbett

All Rights Reserved

Mongol Empire: The Man Behind the Mongol Empire (The History and Legacy of the Mongol Empire's Capital)

ISBN 978-1-77485-806-6

No part of this guidebook shall be reproduced in any form without permission in writing from the publisher except in the case of brief quotations embodied in critical articles or reviews.

Legal & Disclaimer

The information contained in this ebook is not designed to replace or take the place of any form of medicine or professional medical advice. The information in this ebook has been provided for educational & entertainment purposes only.

The information contained in this book has been compiled from sources deemed reliable, and it is accurate to the best of the Author's knowledge; however, the Author cannot guarantee its accuracy and validity and cannot be held liable for any errors or omissions. Changes are periodically made to this book. You must consult your doctor or get professional medical advice before using any of the suggested remedies, techniques, or information in this book.

Upon using the information contained in this book, you agree to hold harmless the Author from and against any damages, costs, and expenses, including any legal fees potentially resulting from the application of any of the information provided by this guide. This disclaimer applies to any damages or injury caused by the use and application, whether directly or indirectly, of any advice or information presented, whether for breach of contract, tort, negligence, personal injury, criminal intent, or under any other cause of action.

You agree to accept all risks of using the information presented inside this book. You need to consult a professional medical practitioner in order to ensure you are both able and healthy enough to participate in this program.

Table Of Contents

Chapter 1: The Mongols And Their Background 1

Chapter 2: The Life And Rise Of The Great Khan 11

Chapter 3: The Mongol Empire 23

Chapter 4: Genghis' Successors.............. 38

Chapter 5: The Final Decades Of Unity And Decline 47

Chapter 6: Legacy And Impact 57

Chapter 7: What The Mongolian Empire Consisted Of.. 67

Chapter 8: The Structure Of The Empire 75

Chapter 9: Union In The Empire 81

Chapter 10: China's Yuan Dynasty.......... 91

Chapter 11: The Empires In Central Asia 103

Chapter 12: In Iran, The Il-Khans 107

Chapter 13: A Tumultuous Childhood .. 113

Chapter 14: Mongolia: A Rich History .. 130

Chapter 15: Uniting Mongolia 148

Chapter 16: Mongolia Under Khan 166

Chapter 1: The Mongols and Their Background

Officially, the Mongol Empire reigned between 1206 and 1368, which is the main period we will focus on throughout this book. However, as is always the case, there was plenty of history that predated these important events and paved the way for the era in question. In the course of that era, the Mongols went from being a number of nomadic steppe tribes to a unified force that would annex numerous other empires and cultures throughout Asia and beyond.

First and foremost, it's important to note that, historically and geographically speaking, "Mongolia" can refer to an area that stretches beyond the borders of the present-day Republic of the same name. The modern country is landlocked between Russia and China to the north and south, respectively. Today's Mongolia corresponds to what has historically been known as Outer Mongolia, while Inner Mongolia, just to the south, is still an autonomous region in China.

Map of Mongolia

Combined with a couple of smaller regions in Russia to the north, these lands can collectively be referred to as the Mongolian Plateau. Another important area is Manchuria, which is a region in present-day China just to the east of Inner Mongolia, north of the Korean Peninsula. Historically, these and other regions toward western China were ruled by rivaling Chinese dynasties, which formed a complex political situation. All the while, various nomadic tribes prowled the steppes to the north, often divided and engaged in intertribal conflict.

Mongol Origins

As you can imagine, many things about the exact origins of the Mongols are uncertain, and we don't know much about them prior to their rise in the 12th century. The most likely scenarios are that the early Mongols were either indigenous Asiatic people on the Mongolian Plateau or descendants of people who moved in from the Siberian steppes at some point.

Be that as it may, traces of human activity not just in Mongolia but all over the Eurasian steppes go back to the Paleolithic Period. During the Stone Age, more than 100,000 years ago, humans were already prowling the southern parts of Mongolia and the Gobi Desert. People continuously inhabited the area since then, and semblances of some early tribal formations began to appear roughly around the 1st millennium BC, although some of the important artifacts found in Outer Mongolia were significantly older. Going as far back as 5,000 years, artifacts, remains of settlements, and various structures such as tombs are throughout Mongolia.

Around 1500 BC, climate changes in this region had a large impact on how local populations developed. Mongolia became colder, and the climate grew increasingly dry, which affected the people's ability to maintain farms. This shift most likely led the nomads in Mongolia to focus on keeping livestock as the main source of food. Certainly, farming and agriculture were known to these people of the plains, but their conditions simply made livestock more viable.

As such, the Mongols and their ancestors are better viewed as herders instead of farmers, with the latter being the most common way of life in much of the known world at the time. Most importantly, the harsh conditions in the steppes made the Mongols tough as nails, and their way of life cultivated the development of certain skills that would later prove crucial for their success. For one, horsemanship was crucial to navigating the open plains, so the Mongols focused on becoming great horsemen. They also selectively bred their horses for speed and agility. On top of that, hunting in the steppes necessitated ranged weapons due to a lack of cover for sneaking and hiding. For this reason, the Mongols became such renowned archers.

According to Chinese historiography, the Mongols, or at least some of their precursor tribes, were initially located around the Ergune River, which is one of the rivers flowing along the present-day Russo-Chinese border. From this locale, the Mongols might have migrated westward into parts of present-day Mongolia in the 7th century, particularly around the rivers Onon, Kerulen, and Tuul.

Ergune River

What would later become the Mongols was probably a loose group of several tribes at that time. When referring to the Mongols as "Mengwu," the Chinese records from that time were talking about just one of the Mongolian tribes. Indeed, the Mongolian Plateau and areas further north, around the Lake Baikal in Russia, were occupied by numerous nomadic tribes, some of which are now well-known, such as the Tatars. Other tribes or, rather, confederations of tribes included the Khamag Mongols, Keraites, Merkits, and others.

Even though loosely related and often warring Mongol tribes were spread over the Mongolian Plateau since as early as 2,000 years BC, they wouldn't really dominate the region for quite a long time. Over the centuries, the Eurasian steppes saw the rise of various peoples like the Scythians, Xiongnu, ancient Turkic peoples, and the Uyghurs.

All in all, it's clear that the Eurasian steppes and the Mongolian Plateau itself was teeming with human activity for millennia. The people who would later be known as the Mongols were merely a drop in the bucket in the grand scheme of things. They moved around, hunted, herded cattle, practiced horsemanship, and looked for suitable pastoral plains. Eventually, their focus tightened on the Mongolian Plateau, and they began to stick around. The Mongols were undoubtedly nomads, but that didn't mean they would move to a different land every week. Their nomadic lifestyle simply meant that they didn't focus much on agriculture and preferred to have the ability to pack up and leave when needed, and they usually did so when it was in their best interest.

Pre-Imperial Context

The time before the unification and the rise of the Mongols coincided with political rivalries, particularly between powerful Chinese dynasties. On top of that, the Chinese were in near constant conflict with the tribes to the north for centuries, particularly over land. The Chinese would often come into direct conflict with early Mongol tribes due to their expansion northward in search of farmland. This expansion forced the tribes to give up quality land and, in turn, they would often conduct raids on Chinese settlers.

From the 10th century onward, the Khitan Liao dynasty ruled a significant area of land in northern China and parts of Manchuria and eastern Mongolia. However, a federation of tribes known as the Jurchens grew stronger in northeastern China and founded the Jin dynasty. The Jurchens crushed the Liao dynasty in 1125 and seized much of their former territories. Taking over as the dominant authority in the area, the Jin dynasty soon came into conflict with the Mongol tribes as well, particularly the Khamag Mongols. The dynasty successfully resisted the Mongol onslaught, however.

Already at this point, the Khamag Mongol confederation emerged as something of a precursor for the latter Mongol state as we know it. The period of the 1130s also marks the first recorded Khan of the Mongols, known as Khabul Khan. Khabul was the Khan of the Khamag Mongols, but if we take this confederation as an early development of Mongol statehood, then he is the first Khan. In fact, Khabul Khan was the great-grandfather of Genghis Khan. Even though the wars against the Jin dynasty weren't very successful for the Khamag Mongols for a time, they undoubtedly became the dominant tribe on the Mongolian Plateau.

However, the early Mongols had two major problems. For one, their wars against the Jin were often wars of attrition and, as such, these conflicts weakened the already comparatively small Khamag Mongol confederation. Secondly, the Jin divide and conquer strategy among the nomadic tribes was still very successful, so the Mongols also had to fight against many tribes that were in a similar situation, notably the Tatars. Another competing power was west of Jin under the Tangut Western Xia Dynasty. To the south of Jin, the Chinese Song Empire was under the famous Song dynasty.

These and many other dynasties along with their respective states comprised much of what is now China and Kazakhstan. All the while, the Mongols, Tatars, Merkits, and other competing, nomadic tribes lay to the north of the main political landscape in the Asian heartland. Indeed, just like much of Asian history, the 12th century was a tumultuous time. The nomadic tribes fought each other, and the important dynasties struggled among themselves for supremacy. At the same time, the empire had to deal with the raiding nomads as well. This situation was a complex landscape of intertribal relations, however, and the different tribes and their confederations did occasionally come together to pursue common goals.

Toward the middle of the 12th century, the Jin dynasty and the Mongols reached an agreement after a Jin initiative to create peace. This time of peace allowed the Mongols to focus on settling their scores with other tribes, especially the Tatars. Prior to this, Mongol-Tatar relations turned sour after a Tatar betrayal that saw the Jin capture and execute Khabul Khan's successor. Therefore, the Tatars and the Mongols warred against each other well into the second half of the 12th century until a united offensive by the Tatars and the Jin inflicted a defeat on the Mongols in 1161.

Nonetheless, the early Mongols persevered and continued to attack, notably in 1205 when they struck against the Western Xia Empire, which would submit to the Mongols just a few short years later. A new day began for the Mongols as they now had one of the greatest war leaders at their helm. Genghis Khan was born just a year after the Tartars and Jin defeated the Mongols, and his life was quite a ride, unfolding throughout these early decades of the Mongol emergence.

Chapter 2: The Life and Rise of the Great Khan

Genghis Khan - Mongolian Emperor

As you can see, the Mongols were strong people who were tempered by adversity and harsh life, but their potential was being squandered due to their disunity. The nearby regional powers were probably wary of these nomads since the start, which was why they did their best to keep the nomads bickering and fighting among themselves. The nearby dynasties knew that if the Mongols were to unite, they would pose a major threat to their dominions. Soon the Mongols would realize their true power and unite to conquer the region, and all it took was one spark to set the process in motion.

Battle between Asian nomad tribes

That spark would come in the form of one special man, whose name would later become synonymous with the Mongols and their empire. That man was Genghis Khan. His successful rule and military conquests have been all but unparalleled in history. Genghis Khan has often been compared to other military leaders in history, such as Napoleon, Alexander the Great, and others, but few have conquered so much land and in such a short time. What's more, Genghis accomplished feats other great conquerors couldn't, such as the conquest of Russia.

Russia has been invaded many times by some of the most powerful armies in history, such as those of Napoleon and Hitler. And yet, neither Napoleon nor Hitler could subdue the Russians, both suffering immensely during the infamous Russian winter. The Mongols, on the other hand, would not be repelled. In fact, the icy winters in Russia often seemed to help the horse-mounted Mongols because they could easily storm across frozen rivers, which have otherwise always been significant natural barriers for armies throughout history.

Early Life

As with other aspects of Mongol history, most of what we know about Genghis' early life comes from outside sources, particularly from China and subsequent European explorers. Because of that, there are some minor disagreements on the facts, but we generally have a fairly accurate idea of the life of Genghis, especially once he rose to power.

Genghis Khan was born as Temujin most likely in 1162 to Yesugei, the leader of the Mongol Borjigin clan, and his wife, Hoelun. His place of birth is located in Burkhan Khaldun, a mountain in the Khentii Province of northeastern Mongolia. Mongol tradition suggests that baby Temujin was born with a blood clot in his fist, which is seen as a sign of destined greatness. Legends also tell us of Temujin's divine origins and his ancestor being a gray wolf. He was his father's eldest son, and the family wasn't very high up in the hierarchy. Temujin's father was a vassal of a more powerful tribal leader, and the family most likely had a tradition in blacksmithing.

The world that Temujin was born into was an unforgiving place that was hard on people in ways that we probably can't fathom nowadays. While Temujin was just a boy at around age nine, his father left him to live with the family of his future wife, according to a marriage arrangement. Like most Mongol boys, Temujin was expected to marry at the age of twelve, being a servant to the head of the family until that time. He also grew up with three brothers, two half-brothers, and a sister.

Not long after this arrangement, Temujin's father was killed by Tatars in an act of retaliation for their earlier conflicts. As the eldest son, Temujin was due to become the head of the Borjigin clan, but his young age discouraged support, and the family was soon abandoned. The rival Taychiut family used this opportunity to take over control of the entire clan. The following years were a time of great hardship for Temujin and his family who were now forced to live the nomadic lifestyle all by their lonesome, often struggling just to eat.

Temujin had to grow up quickly, so he practiced hunting, riding, and fighting, showing great promise. However, in his youth, Temujin showed his belligerent, ruthless side as well. Written legend has it that Temujin killed one of his half-brothers during a seemingly unimportant altercation. While this act was met with shock and great disapproval from his mother, it also consolidated Temujin as the head of his family.

Sometime later, most likely around 1182, Temujin spent some time in captivity and enslavement when the Taychiut captured him. By this time,

Temujin already had ambitions, particularly within his former clan. Over time, he also attracted some supporters thanks to his charisma and adeptness at communication. He was also armed with valuable knowledge and lessons bestowed upon him by his mother, who taught him the value of alliances as a means of navigating the harsh political waters of tribal Mongolia.

As the story goes, Temujin's enslavement didn't last long. On the first night when he attempted to escape, he received help from one of the guards who saw him but, instead of apprehending him, decided to join Temujin's cause. Stories of Temujin's life tell us of multiple such examples where Temujin's personality and drive impressed the people he met, motivating them to join him.

Ultimately, Temujin did marry his arranged wife, Borte of the tribe Konkirat, when he was around sixteen. However, bitter about Temujin's father's earlier transgressions against them, the Merkit tribe kidnapped Temujin's wife. In fact, Temujin's own mother, Hoelun, was a woman whom Yesugei had kidnapped from the Merkit before

Temujin was born. Such was life in the Mongolian steppes during that time.

Temujin reacted quickly to the kidnapping of his wife. He elicited the help of the Keraites, whose Toghril Khan, also known as Ong Khan, had an oath of allegiance to Temujin's father. Toghril was a powerful man who wielded significant forces and political influence, and this allegiance changed Temujin's life forever. On top of helping Temujin recover his wife, Borte, Ong Khan also pledged to help Temujin reunite his former clan and take his rightful position as its leader. Ong Khan assembled thousands of men, and with the addition of the forces commanded by Temujin's childhood friend, Jamuka, they created a significant army.

Mongol army at rest

Needless to say, Temujin brought his wife back safe and mostly unharmed, and she gave birth to his firstborn son a few months later, naming him Jochi. Although Temujin would later have many wives, as per Mongol polygamous tradition at the time, Borte would serve as his empress. Temujin then made an "anda," or blood brother oath, with Jamuka just like his father and Ong Khan did before him. From this point onward, the race was on to subdue the other tribes and bring all the Mongols together under a single banner.

Mongol Unification

Of course, power sharing rarely works out, and there could be only one true Great Khan, so alliances became strained very quickly. For a while, this alliance was very strong and old rivals such as the Merkits would be crushed repeatedly in the ensuing wars. Temujin grew more powerful and influential each day thanks to his successes and his attractive personality.

Temujin's rise attracted negative attention fairly quickly, particularly from Ong Khan's son, Senggum, who began to plot an assassination against Temujin. Unfortunately, Ong Khan took his son's side and the relationship between him and Temujin grew colder. Temujin was well aware of the animosity and the plots, and he and Senggum would soon face off in open combat, where Temujin was repeatedly victorious.

To add insult to injury, Ong Khan later declined to marry one of his daughters to Temujin's son, Jochi, which was a major offense both to Mongol customs and to the alliance itself. A final split soon occurred between the two war leaders and Jamuka, Temujin's closest friend and confidant, chose Ong Khan's side. Once Temujin and his old friend parted ways, however, a significant portion of Jamuka's forces defected to Temujin.

Standing on his own, the future Genghis Khan was, by this point, already a warlord to be reckoned with. Even though Jamuka became estranged from Temujin and began to lean toward Ong Khan, the two didn't get along very well. Because of this and other factors, Temujin would ultimately crush Ong Khan and eventually destroy the Kerait tribe. All the while, Temujin was implementing a clever strategy wherein he would essentially buy people off with promises of great riches and spoils in the victories to come. Coupled with his successes and his charisma, many people agreed to submit, often without a fight.

Already by around 1190, Temujin had united most of the tribes that identified with the Mongol identity up to that point. This unification meant that he had a formidable and, most importantly, loyal force at his back. To feed and support this growing army, Temujin raided many surrounding tribes, inspiring terror far and wide. Many would simply surrender and pledge their allegiances while others had to be beaten into submission. Stories of Temujin's unstoppable war party spread quickly, reducing the number of potential challengers every day.

Genghis Khan at war

With the Keraites out of the way and a good part of the Mongols consolidated behind him, Temujin sought to bring more tribes under his umbrella or destroy them. Another longtime rival was the tribe of Naimans, located to the west of the Mongols. Not only were the Naimans a threat beforehand but they now also had Jamuka on their side. Nonetheless, the indomitable Temujin crushed the Naimans as well as the Tatars in the end.

With each victory, Temujin made sure that he killed the nobility of the defeated tribes and anyone else who wielded political influence. These people, in his mind, were the carriers of old divisions and would surely be able to regroup their supporters at some point to instigate rebellions. After taking out such individuals, Temujin would incorporate all the soldiers and the common folk that he could into his Mongol tribes. Any old roots and ties to previous clan loyalties were cut, as Temujin was forging a new identity in the steppes – one that would bring all the nomads under a single banner and name.

However, in 1201, a Mongol political council, known as the Kurultai, was held with an undesirable outcome for Temujin. These gatherings were meetings of khans and other important tribal leaders, which served as a means of making certain decisions in Mongolia. The one in 1201 ended with Jamuka being proclaimed the Gur Khan, or "Universal Ruler," by the khans still loyal to him.

Temujin and Jamuka had been at odds for some time up to that point, but this proclamation drew the battle lines clearer than ever. A final showdown, which would determine the supreme leader of all the Mongols once and for all, was now imminent. Those tribal leaders who had paid attention to the unfolding events and could think ahead were quick to defect to Temujin's side. While Jamuka did form a sizeable coalition, Temujin's influence and popularity grew constantly.

Politically savvy people throughout the Mongolian Plateau were probably well aware of what was going on in the great scheme of things. It was becoming clearer that a great process of unification was afoot, and that only one man could emerge as the ruler of the steppes. Among those who switched camp to Temujin was Subutai, the brother of Jelme, a general who was one of Temujin's closest confidants.

The war would go on for a few years, and while Temujin did suffer some setbacks against Jamuka, he ultimately came out on top. Jamuka was betrayed and brought before Temujin as a captive around 1206. As legend has it, Temujin did offer a renewal of friendship to Jamuka, but the man refused it, acknowledging that there can be only one Great Khan and that Temujin had proved himself to be the greater man. He was given a noble death and the vast majority of his coalition submitted to Temujin. That same year, Temujin called a new Kurultai council and was finally proclaimed the Great Khan, taking the name and title of Genghis Khan.

Coronation of Genghis Khan

In all, Genghis Khan crushed the Merkits, Keraites, Tatars, Uyghurs, Naimans, and many other Mongol and Turkic tribes and confederations. Despite his ruthlessness, Genghis' charisma and leadership skills made him widely beloved, especially among the commoners he would integrate into his tribe. He also established a sort of meritocracy in that his inner circle men were appointed based on achievement and merit, not blood relations or name. And so, in 1206, Genghis Khan ascended as the sole great leader on the Mongolian Plateau, a renewed Mongol identity was forged from all the conquered and allied tribes, and the Mongol Empire was born.

Chapter 3: The Mongol Empire

Genghis Khan monument

What is born must also grow, of course, and so the period from 1206 onward was a time of glorious as well as brutal expansion for the Mongols. Before that, however, Genghis Khan focused on consolidating his realm, appointing all the right people to important positions, expanding his family, and building an even stronger army.

This period also shows us the intelligence and sophistication of Genghis Khan's state building, as told in the Secret History of the Mongols. This monumental piece of literature is the oldest preserved Mongol writing, which was created not long after Genghis passed away in 1227. This book is an invaluable piece of history of great importance to the Mongol nation and a major source for many things we know about the Mongols. The Secret History chronicles the life and exploits of Genghis Khan, but it also tells us much more about Mongol society in general.

The imperial stage of the Mongols lasted for a shorter time than other world's empires, but they managed to break the mold, innovate, and impress in many ways. Their cleverness, effectiveness, place of origin, and the speed with which they conquered half the world are all reasons why some people refer to the Mongols as one of history's greatest anomalies.

Consolidation

Sources vary, but most agree that Genghis Khan was most likely the ruler of around one to two-million people once his process of unification was finalized. Victory at war was only half the battle, however, as Genghis Khan now had to smash an entire system of undesirable traditions, outlooks, and values. The highly tribal and conflict-prone Mongolian Plateau could not change overnight just because one man won a bunch of battles.

Still, thanks to Genghis' example, everyone began to realize what could be accomplished if people gathered around a competent leader, set their petty conflicts aside, and stuck to their loyalties. The old system of tribes and clans was slowly but surely going extinct. The central ruler now had such a large following that those folks who still wanted to separate and run their own competing tribes simply found it wasn't worth their while anymore.

One of the innovations Genghis made was to extend his previous meritocratic ideas to most facets of society, not just his inner circle. Many aristocratic titles were abolished, and aristocrats who were suspected future rebels or troublemakers were quickly removed to be replaced by competent men deemed right for the job. Most of the time under Genghis Khan, competence was valued over nepotism, which is the practice of favoring one's kin regardless of qualification. Furthermore, Genghis Khan outlawed the enslavement of other Mongols as well as the old practices of kidnapping and selling women. Theft of the most important Mongol resource – livestock – was now an offense that could yield the death penalty.

Perhaps more importantly, however, Genghis Khan soon ordered a writing system be introduced so that the predominantly illiterate Mongols could begin to record information and educate themselves about the world. This decision shows us that Genghis thought ahead and that, to him, empire building was more than just land-grabbing. Genghis also instructed the empire's leadership to start conducting population censuses, and he introduced a system of diplomatic immunity for the ambassadors of foreign powers in Mongolia.

Ancient Mongolian parchment

During Genghis Khan's reign, the Mongols began their policy of religious tolerance toward the people they conquered. As long as they submitted to the new order, paid their tributes, and didn't cause trouble, newly incorporated populations were mostly left alone and allowed to maintain their cultural identity. This approach was incredibly progressive for that time, especially in contrast to places like Europe.

The vast majority of European countries were very stringently Christian and dogmatic. Putting aside the moral aspects of religious suppression, this mindset had other negative consequences in Europe. Dogmatism discouraged innovation and the emergence of new, useful ideas, which was one of the reasons why many important inventions in Europe made their way there from Asia, thanks to the Mongols.

Overall, Genghis Khan formed a sort of military and civil code that would govern Mongol politics and life for a long time to come. This system, called the Yassa code, was a unified code that would govern all the Mongol lands in an equal way. While its existence has been confirmed, the written code itself has never been found, so we only know those details that were outlined in other writings and oral traditions.

For instance, things like aristocracy, the upper echelons of society, weren't abolished, but both the aristocrats and the common folk were given clear roles in society, which meant both rights and obligations. The Yassa also listed other specific laws. The Mongol postal system, stretching far across the empire at all times and relying on messengers to quickly spread information and goods, was given special attention. The messengers employed in this service were protected, so disturbing or harming them in any way was a great crime.

Furthermore, while, as we mentioned, the Mongol social mobility and ranks were greatly based on merits, Genghis Khan's family was still enjoying a special status. His family enjoyed great riches thanks to the subsequent conquests, and Genghis expanded the family for a long time with many different wives, although his first wife, Borte, was the most important. He had four sons with her, and all of them were given regions to govern in the realm once they came of age. The highest authority in the country was certainly reserved for members of his Golden Family, as prescribed by Yassa.

Still, this was definitely the 13th century, and the Mongol conquests were undoubtedly often marked by brutality. Although they practiced their indigenous forms of shamanism, the Mongols weren't focused heavily on religion or race and ethnicity for that matter. Nonetheless, those who resisted in any way, such as Muslims in some regions, were utterly destroyed. The Mongols also used forced labor and threw many conquered folks into slavery, taking their women for themselves and desecrating entire civilizations. These things almost never happened to those who chose to integrate peacefully, though.

Social engineering and politics aside, the Mongol society was still one built for war, focused primarily on the military. Genghis Khan used a decimal system to divvy up his forces into well-organized fighting units. Discipline and intense military training were crucial, and Genghis made sure that these standards were kept. On top of that, the military could never lack for anything – they had to be fed properly and well-equipped.

Mongolian war equipment

The real power of the Khan's army, however, was his ability to select the right people for the top slots in his army. Genghis Khan's top generals were usually either his sons or men who had proven themselves as staunch loyalists for years in the field. On top of all that, the generals were competent and judged by the Khan as qualified for the job. This combination of loyalty and skill ensured the cohesion and effectiveness of the army.

Genghis himself was a brilliant and, most importantly, adaptable military mind. His cavalry-based forces dominated the steppes, of course, but later on in his conquests, Genghis was up against tactics and military scenarios largely foreign to the Mongols. A particular issue was the people whom the Mongols would later fight were sedentary, living in fixed locations in walled-off cities. Genghis Khan's horse-mounted, steppe-prowling ways could not apply to besieging a city. Nonetheless, the Mongols quickly adapted and overcame these obstacles. Wherever the Khan would go, he would learn and immediately adopt something new. This flexibility ultimately led the Mongols to use catapults, siege construction, boiling hot oil, explosives, and many other things that enabled them to lay waste to cities.

With the competition neutralized and the newborn Mongol state firmly in place, Genghis Khan could finally turn his attention to the ambitions beyond the borders. As legends tell us, Genghis Khan's dreams were constantly haunted by visions of great and glorious conquests in new, uncharted lands, especially those beyond the formidable walls built by the Chinese to keep the nomads such as him out. Genghis Khan felt it was time to pursue his true destiny, and the horde was ready.

Genghis Khan's Conquests

During much of Genghis Khan's rise to power, neighboring realms such as the Jin dynasty didn't pay much heed to the man. The Jin engaged in their usual politics and plots, trying to play the nomadic tribes against one another and probably underestimating Genghis Khan a great deal. In fact, during their wars with the Tatars, the Jin dynasty called upon Temujin to help them crush the constantly invading Tatars, which he did with great success.

As such, Genghis' military prowess was known far and wide sometime before he became the Great Khan in 1206. Nonetheless, the Jin dynasty still felt Genghis Khan would be largely inconsequential to their supremacy in the region. Indeed, Genghis Khan was very busy subduing the other nomadic tribes, and he really didn't pose a major threat to the Jin Empire for a while. Once he won and unified the Mongols, however, things would never be the same.

As Genghis Khan assumed his title in 1206, the hostilities with the Western Xia realm in northwestern China were already well underway. This major campaign would be the first Genghis

Khan undertook outside the bounds of Mongolia. For the first few years, the conflict consisted largely of Mongol raids against the kingdom until 1209, when the Mongols fully committed to conquering them.

Genghis Khan's real goal from the start was China beyond the Great Wall, particularly the Jin dynasty to the south and east. However, the Western Xia was a threat that could strike from behind, so Genghis decided to neutralize them and secure his flank before new conquests. Genghis was also well-informed on the situation in both of these realms, knowing a young and inexperienced ruler headed the Jin dynasty at the time. This situation led Genghis to believe Jin wouldn't get involved if he attacked the Tangut Xia realm, and he was right.

Great Wall of China

Using newly adopted siege tactics, the Mongols quickly made their way to the gates of Yinchuan, the Xia capital. According to some sources, the Mongols even tried to divert a nearby river and flood the city instead of fighting, but this attempt failed. Nonetheless, the pressure caused by the thousands of battle-hardened Mongol horsemen was enough to force the Xia rulers to submit already in 1209.

This crushing victory propelled the Mongol horde to new heights. The Jin dynasty, however, quite foolishly decided to demand Genghis Khan's formal submission to their rule. As you have learned earlier, the Jin dynasty had a long history of meddling with Mongolian affairs, and they were effectively overlords of all the northern nomads for the most part. Things were changing irreversibly throughout the Mongolian Plateau and China, though, but the Jin dynasty didn't seem to get that memo.

Genghis decided he was ready in 1211, and he began to wage war against the Jin. During one of the first engagements, the ever-confident Jurchens sent a messenger, Ming-Tan, with demands to Genghis Khan's army instead of attacking first. The messenger quickly defected and gave away important information to Genghis, letting him know exactly where the Jin forces were waiting for them. What ensued was the Battle of Yehuling, or the Battle of Wild Fox Ridge, where the Jin army was utterly destroyed by

September, although the Mongols suffered great casualties as well.

Over the next couple of years, Genghis Khan left a trail of destruction and desolation throughout the Jin borderlands. Jin cities deeper inside the country were forced to accept thousands of refugees, which put a great strain on their economies, leading to famine. Shortages of supplies forced the Jin armies to massacre many of their own people to contain the famine. The formerly subjugated Mongol nomads were wreaking havoc in the once mighty Jin realm, and the kingdom was in shambles.

Not even the Great Wall of China could keep the Mongols out, and they crossed the barrier in 1213, moving further into the country. After a string of victories, Genghis Khan laid siege to the Jin capital of Zhongdu (present-day Beijing) in 1214. Initially, the Jin emperor agreed to pay great tribute in silk, gold, silver, horses, and much more. The tribute was part of a submission agreement that subordinated the Jin to Genghis and guaranteed a cessation of hostilities. However, the Jin decided to move their capital to the south instead, which prompted a merciless reaction from Genghis. The Mongols quickly captured, sacked, and utterly destroyed Zhongdu shortly thereafter.

Genghis Khan soon began to spread out his campaigns across multiple fronts by sending his most competent and trusted generals in numerous directions. During the aforementioned campaign against the Jin dynasty, Genghis sent Jebe, or "the Arrow," to subdue the remnants of the already defeated Naiman confederation, whose khan was now rebelling. The rebellious khan took over the Khanate of Kara-Khitan, which was friendly to Genghis. The competent general Jebe made short work of this task, and the Mongol empire incorporated Kara-Khitan. By 1218, Genghis Khan had expanded his realm all the way to Lake Balkhash in present-day eastern Kazakhstan. The Mongols now bordered Khwarazm, which was a Muslim empire stretching across present-day Turkmenistan, Afghanistan, Uzbekistan, and Iran.

Map including Lake Balkhash, Turkmenistan, Uzbekistan, and Kazakhstan

At this time, Genghis Khan didn't want to invade Khwarazm yet and instead sought to enter a trade agreement with them. The agreement was reached, but a local governor attacked and robbed the first trade caravan that arrived in Khwarazm, and its Muslim traders were massacred. These people were under Genghis Khan's protection, and so this attack was a sign of great disrespect and direct challenge. To add insult to injury, the Khwarazm ruler, Shah Ala ad-Din Muhammad II, denied Genghis compensation. On top of that, the diplomats Genghis then sent to negotiate were executed. Genghis Khan then mobilized his army, left his general, Muqali, in charge of pacifying the other rivals in China, and marched on Khwarazm.

Statues of two generals of Genghis Khan at the Government Palace

Khwarazm had brought upon itself the most destructive storm of Mongol fury, and the ensuing war was a spectacle of sheer brutality and destruction. Genghis stormed through the Islamic empire, pillaging, burning, and destroying cities one after another. Cities such a Samarkand,

Urgench, and Bukhara were ravaged, with resisting soldiers, unskilled commoners, and aristocrats massacred or enslaved. In their usual fashion, the Mongols took in those folks whose skills they found useful, but the others were either killed or used as human shields.

By 1223, the Khwarazm lands were in ruins and littered with well over a million corpses. This war of terror was the ultimate testament to the Mongol reputation, and it cemented them as the most ferocious warring horde in the lands. Genghis Khan's dominion now stretched from the Sea of Japan to the Caspian Sea, virtually across all of Asia.

Chapter 4: Genghis' Successors

Before Genghis Khan gathered his forces and left Khwarazm, he proclaimed his son Ogedei as his heir and successor. He devised a simple system of succession, which stated that all succeeding khans had to be his descendants. After that, the Mongol army was split in two, and Genghis led one part of it in raids throughout India and Afghanistan while Jebe and Subutai attacked locations in the Caucasus and present-day Russia. As usual, anyone who mounted any resistance was crushed, and the Mongols added Persia and Transoxiana to their empire. The entirety of the Mongol horde began to head home in 1225.

The Khan's Final Years

The Mongols came into hostile contact with numerous different peoples on their way back to Mongolia. After defeating the Georgians, other armies in Azerbaijan, and elsewhere around the Caspian Sea, a detachment led by Jebe and Subutai spent the winter near the Black Sea.

The Mongols later clashed with the forces of Kievan Rus, notably in the Battle of the Kalka

River in 1223. Other forces from the region supplemented the Kievan army, forming a coalition against the Mongols. It was to no avail, however, and the Mongols were victorious once again. Even though the Mongols then signed a peace deal with the Russians, the people of nobility were executed as usual.

One notable defeat the Mongols suffered during this time was at the hands of the Volga Bulgars, but soon the Mongols returned and crushed them on a second attempt, conquering Volga Bulgaria and laying down the foundation of what would later become the Golden Horde. In the end, the Mongols defeated everyone in their path and established their dominion around the entirety of the Caspian Sea.

Once Genghis Khan and his horde were back in Mongolia, Genghis set his sights on unfinished business in the neighborhood. While Genghis was campaigning in Khwarazm, the vassals in Western Xia refused to pledge their share of the forces to support the invasion, perhaps thinking that Genghis Khan would suffer a defeat against the Muslim forces. Not only that, but the Xia Tanguts joined forces with the remnants of the Jin dynasty and formed an alliance to defeat the Mongols.

Mongolian infantry warrior

This disobedience wasn't something that Genghis Khan could let go unpunished, so he focused on ending this resistance once and for all in one, final attack. The war began in 1226 and, during that year, Tangut cities and strongholds fell one after another. The Mongols attacked the Western Xia capital in 1227, promptly capturing it and pressing on until the last bits of resistance were extinguished. The Tanguts mounted a significant resistance and fought hard, but they were no match for the battle-hardened, overwhelming Mongol horde. The Western Xia Empire surrendered that same year, which brought an end to their 189 years of dominion. Seeing no value in keeping around the aristocracy that betrayed him many times, Genghis Khan slaughtered the ruling dynasty.

Genghis was well aware of two important things. First and foremost, he knew an empire as vast as his could not last under just one ruler and without any kind of decentralization. Secondly, like all intelligent war leaders, he knew any day could be his last. Because of these concerns, Genghis divided up his empire into a few khanates that would be ruled by regional rulers made up of his sons and grandsons. These rulers were supposed to be subordinate to the Great Khan, Genghis' own direct successor, Ogedei Khan. This idea later led to the formation of different Mongol khanates, some of which would continue to rule their regions for centuries after Genghis Khan.

Genghis Khan died during the last days of Xia resistance, on August 18, 1227. The death of such a glorious leader was a monumental event, so it spawned quite a bit of folklore and legend. Because of this, history isn't certain on the details of Genghis' death. A common account is the one where he fell off a horse due to fatigue, suffering an internal injury. He is said to have continued to lead his army but ultimately succumbed to his injury and died in his sleep.

As per the Great Khan's request, he was buried in an unmarked grave that has never been found. As in life, legends surrounded Genghis in death as well. Mongol folklore talks about the burial in great detail. Folks said that the mighty funeral party, consisting of fierce warriors most loyal to the Great Khan, killed all witnesses to the funeral.

Genghis Khan mausoleum near Ordos, Inner Mongolia, China

Troubled Successions

Genghis Khan was survived by many children and a massive, elite army. The Mongol cavalry and other forces had come a long way since Genghis' humble beginnings. This army was no rugged band of raiders anymore; Genghis' cavalry was elite, well-equipped, well-trained, highly experienced, and battle-hardened. These horsemen constituted a great chunk of the total army, which, at the time of Genghis' death, numbered close to 130,000 men. These forces were shared and assigned to the command of the Great Khan's sons, grandsons, and other relatives.

Genghis' successor, Ogedei Khan, was a successful ruler who reigned between 1229 and 1241. He established his seat of power at Karakorum in central Mongolia, which would serve as the capital between 1235 and 1260. Incredibly enough, the Mongol conquests not only continued but intensified during this time. Some historians believe the Mongols became even more ferocious after the death of their first Great Khan. By the time the Mongols finished off Western Xia later in 1227, this civilization was all but exterminated.

Under Ogedei, the Mongols seized lands deep inside Persia, crushed the last remaining Khwarazmids, and finally came into contact with the Chinese Song dynasty in the southeast. Of course, this contact was very quickly marked by hostilities, and it was the beginning of a prolonged period of warfare between the two powers, which would last all the way until 1279.

In the late 1230s, the Mongols focused even more on invading the farther reaches of Russia and Europe. These attacks were led by Batu Khan, the ruler of the Blue Horde, one of the sub-regions, as envisioned by Genghis Khan. The Mongols thus carved a path into Central Europe as well. By 1241, Batu Khan and general Subutai were fighting Poles, Germans, and Hungarians, creating vassals almost everywhere they went. These Mongol forces stopped at Vienna and return to

Mongolia in 1241 when news broke that Ogedei Khan had died.

What ensued was a troubled period and a succession crisis, where Ogedei's widow ruled over the empire as a regent for five years. There were rivalries between many of Genghis' grandsons and the integrity of the empire began to waver. After this five-year regency, Ogedei's widow managed to appoint her son, Guyuk Khan as the ruler. However, Guyuk's tenure as the Great Khan was short-lived and sometimes challenged, particularly by Batu Khan, who refused to acknowledge his authority. Guyuk died in 1248, paving the way for another three years of regency and instability.

A degree of stability returned to the Mongol Empire with the ascension of Mongke Khan, who ruled until 1259. The Mongol Empire was becoming an even more interesting place by this time, being influenced by all the cultures they came into contact with. European accounts from the capital Karakorum in 1254 spoke of churches, mosques, and Buddhist temples being built one next to another.

By most accounts, Mongke was a good and kind ruler to his people, but he too managed to expand the empire further with the help of his two brothers, Hulegu and Kublai. During this time, the Mongols conquered great portions of present-day Iran and Iraq and sacked the city of Baghdad in 1258, which served as the capital of the mighty Abbasid Caliphate during that time.

Hulegu Khan mobilized his forces for conquest in present-day Syria in 1259. The initial attacks were successful as usual, and the Mongols had now reached the Mediterranean, preparing to strike southward into Palestine and then Egypt, with the ultimate goal being the domination of North Africa. However, the Mongols finally met their match when they clashed with Egyptian Mamluks, many of whom were enslaved Slavs with valuable experience in fighting the Mongols earlier. On top of that, the bulk of the Mongol forces had already withdrawn back to Mongolia after news of Mongke Khan's death in 1259. The Mongols were defeated at the Battle of Ayn Jalut in 1260 and, for the first time in history, didn't return with a vengeance.

A statue of Kublai Khan at a government palace

Already in 1260, Kublai had secured his spot as the next Great Khan via a vote while he was campaigning in China, although the succession was challenged once again. The main competing claimant was Arigboge, Kublai's younger brother in the capital Karakorum. Hulegu, who was at that time still campaigning in Syria, would later come into conflict with Kublai and Hulegu's cousin, Berke.

While Kublai was mostly recognized as the Great Khan, fractures began to show throughout the empire. The state was perhaps too vast and diverse to control for long. Nonetheless, the period roughly between 1250 and 1350 would come to be known as the Century of Peace, or Pax Mongolica. The Mongol conquests brought about a relative peace in the grand scheme of things and a connection between the eastern and western worlds, facilitating trade like never before.

Chapter 5: The Final Decades of Unity and Decline

As we mentioned earlier, Genghis' will was for the empire to be split up into subregions subordinate to the central authority of the Great Khan. From a political standpoint, this move was necessary, but then again, it also meant that the lines for separation and disintegration were set. The main khanates to emerge were the Blue and White Horde khanates, which later became the Golden Horde under Batu Khan, Il-Khanate (Hulegu), Empire of the Great Khan in China (Kublai), Mongol heartland with Karakorum (Tolui), and Chagatai Khanate, ruled by Chagatai.

Street view of the city and the gate of the Palace of the Khan of the capital city of Golden Horde Sarai-Batu

The vast empire was divided between a few very powerful people and their successors. The different khanates were mostly under the rule of Genghis Khan's sons, grandsons, and relatives, but rivalries would emerge nonetheless.

Kublai Khan

Despite the emerging issues, Kublai Khan was undoubtedly one of the greatest Mongol leaders, as well as the last Great Khan to be universally recognized. Because of his dispute with his brother, Arigboge, Kublai established his own capital in Khanbaliq, present-day Beijing. Kublai made this move in 1260 and would initiate reconstruction projects in the city during 1267. Here, Kublai would begin to identify more and more with being a Chinese emperor.

It would seem this immersion was something of a trend throughout the Mongol Empire during Kublai Khan's rule. Namely, regional khans, and with them their followers, began to absorb more influence from the vastly diverse people the Mongols conquered. Some converted from Mongol shamanism and other traditional religious practices to Islam, Christianity, Buddhism, and the like. This factor was perhaps one that contributed to the eventual fragmentation of the empire.

Kublai Khan hunting, transported in a palanquin carried by four caparisoned elephants

Between 1260 and 1264, Kublai managed to defeat his younger brother in battle during a war of succession known as the Toluid Civil War, named after the Tolui family, which both the brothers belonged to. Ten years and many successful conquests later, Kublai Khan was the first Great Khan who attempted to invade the Japanese archipelago. Japan was a tough nut to crack, however, thanks to its isolation. Despite hundreds upon hundreds of ships, the invasion failed because the armada was struck by typhoons.

Japanese Warriors Repel Mongol Invasion

In 1279, Kublai was able to finally crush the last remnants of the Chinese Song dynasty after more than forty years of warfare started by Ogedei Khan. He established the Yuan dynasty some years before that, which was essentially Mongol rule in China. This move gave birth to a Mongol-Chinese empire that would last well into the 14th century. Even as such, Kublai Khan is remembered as one of the greatest rulers in the long Chinese history.

Mongol Empire Genghis Khan

Kublai strayed further and further from his Mongol identity, however, which drew a wedge between his realm and the western khanates.

Kublai's culture essentially became Chinese over time. What's more, once he defeated and conquered the Song Empire, Kublai didn't initiate the typical slaughter of aristocracy. He sought to have them under his control, probably as a means of giving legitimacy to his rule over the native Chinese folk. He also ensured that, once the fighting was done, his army didn't pillage and plunder.

Nonetheless, Kublai did initiate certain discriminatory measures against the Han Chinese nobility, stripping them of titles and riches when he saw fit. China had other ethnic groups as well, which Kublai promoted and favored over the Han Chinese. Despite being a foreign conqueror, Kublai revitalized and improved China in many ways, particularly in the areas of economy and infrastructure. During the 1270s, the famous European explorer, Marco Polo, visited these lands. He brought back stories of incredibly advanced culture and civilization, both in regards to old China and the Mongol rule. In fact, Marco Polo's tales were so incredible that many in Europe labeled him a fraud, only to later learn that everything he said was the truth.

Bust statue of Marco Polo, in Villa Borghese Park, Rome

In addition to Japan, Kublai also tried and failed to conquer Dali in present-day southwestern China and Vietnam. In 1281, Kublai tried once again to invade Japan with hundreds of ships and tens of thousands of men. The Mongols engaged in some bitter fighting with Japanese Samurai warriors, but, incredibly enough, the Mongols were once again beset by treacherous weather, ultimately failing to conquer Japan.

Kublai Khan's attempted invasion of Japan in 1281

Kublai Khan died in 1294. He managed to accomplish quite a lot, most notably a firm and secure Mongol hold on the entirety of China. He was the last true Great Khan and remains one of the greatest Mongol rulers, even though some aspects of his reign probably contributed to the eventual total disintegration of the realm. Kublai Khan's rule was the last time the old Mongol Empire would function as a whole. After his death, four distinct khanates were consolidated: the Golden Horde, Il-Khanate, Chagatai Khanate, and the Yuan Dynasty.

Over time, these khanates would drift further and further apart, each wanting to pursue its own destiny, often with little regard to the customs of Genghis Khan's Mongol Empire.

Disintegration

With the disintegration of the Mongol Empire well underway and growing schisms between the interests of the mostly independent khanates, keeping the Silk Road open became more difficult. This historically crucial trading route between the East and the West was kept alive thanks to the security guarantees provided by the Mongol Empire, so the period was referred to as Pax Mongolica, or Mongol Peace. Despite all the constant conquests and warfare, the one thing that could be counted on by all of Eurasia was the

Silk Road. With the death of Kublai, however, the Silk Road's future seemed grim.

The Silk Road

Kublai Khan's rule over in the Yuan Dynasty was succeeded by his grandson, Temur, who ruled between 1295 and 1307. He wasn't the Great Khan, however, as the position was all but abolished in practice. Temur had to maintain Mongol rule over China but also deal with attacks from other Mongols, particularly those from Genghis Khan's lineage. He successfully defended the realm from these attacks and from domestic rivals, though, so his rule was very successful.

Successions throughout the Mongolian and Chinese parts of the empire became increasingly chaotic into the 14th century. During all this time, Kublai's cousins, Batu and Berke, in the Golden Horde and his brother, Hulegu, in Persia grew stronger and more independent. Even though its authority over the western khanates dwindled, the Yuan Dynasty would persist until 1368 on its home grounds. The last Great Khan, even if in name only, was Toghon Temur, and he ruled between 1333 and 1368. Toghon Temur acquired this title when he was only thirteen and history has recorded him as an overall weak and ineffective ruler.

Until Toghon came of age, control over the empire was given to the regency of Bayan, even though his policies were often very detrimental to the Chinese. Native Chinese elites had already been growing their hatreds for a long time, but this period deepened the divide. Chinese nobility grew increasingly weary of the Mongols. Toghon Temur's rule as khan came to an end in 1368 when a rebelling Chinese ex-monk, Zhu Chongba, drove the Mongol ruler out of Beijing. This end was the birth of the famous Chinese dynasty called Ming, and the Mongol hold over China was thus brought to an end. Official history holds 1368 as the year when the Mongol Empire officially ended.

In the coming years, the Ming still fought many wars against the Mongols. The Mongols formed the Northern Yuan Dynasty to continue the struggle, but that one was also crushed around 1382. During this time, the Chinese assimilated all of the Mongol nobles who remained in the country, which meant they had to change their names and customs to fully integrate into the Chinese identity. China also purged the foreign religions from their land, particularly Christianity and, to a great extent, Islam. From this point on, the relationship between China and the Mongols on the Mongolian Plateau mostly reverted back to what it was during the times of the Jin. The Chinese formed a frontier toward the nomads and tried, albeit unsuccessfully, to conquer all of Mongolia.

Elsewhere in Eurasia, however, the other legacy empires continued to exist, some longer than others. The Il-Khanate in Persia, for instance, had been developing along a different path while all of this was happening in China. The Khan of this realm converted to Islam in the late 13th century, changing the whole orientation of the khanate. This country had very little to do with the original Mongol Empire, and their Mongol identity was simply dissolved by the 15th century. The khanate was conquered by Timur along with most of Persia in 1383.

In Central Asia and Russia, the Golden Horde officially persisted until the early 16th century, but its influence diminished all the time. Unified in a desire to rid themselves of Mongol rule, the local Russian and other Slavic nobles eventually gained their independence. The Chagatai Khanate, which was located across present-day eastern Kazakhstan and a number of other countries in the region, was split into eastern and western portions during the 14th century, and the eastern portion lasted until the latter 17th century, although drastically changed and much more Turkic than Mongol.

Even though it fell apart in fewer than two centuries, the Mongol Empire impacted the world on an unprecedented scale. The legacy of Genghis Khan continues to impress, and its signs are everywhere. Genetic studies have shown that 1 in roughly 200 men today carry Genghis Khan's genes. What's more, this mere herder from the steppes made himself the great leader of dissociated nomadic tribes and created an entire nation, which still exists. There are between 10 and 11 million Mongols living on the Mongolian Plateau to this day, carrying and keeping alive the legacy of their Great Khan and once unstoppable empire.

Chapter 6: Legacy and Impact

As you have seen throughout our examination of all this important history, there was a lot of warfare and conquest. However, throughout our chronicles about the Mongols, you were also able to see the other aspects of their empire and of the Mongols as a people. As such, the Mongols have made quite a legacy for themselves and they have been pioneers in many fields. In this chapter, we will take a quick look at a few more important inventions, contributions, achievements, and the ways in which the Mongols have affected our world.

Trade

The period of relative stability and peace during the Pax Mongolica meant a lot more than just a cessation of total warfare. This stability facilitated trade and, thanks to the sheer vastness of the Mongol Empire, distant regions were connected and able to transfer all sorts of goods from one end to the other. The Silk Road provided a venue for commerce between China and Europe. These two regions were very different, and Europe had much to gain from the advanced civilization in China.

People used the Silk Road to share much more than just raw goods. The flow of ideas was just as, if not more important than material resources. Not only were these regions connected, but the trading routes were also kept very safe and secure, especially by medieval standards. According to popular wisdom at the time, one could traverse the Mongol Empire on foot, carrying a golden plate on his head, without worrying for his safety. The security and prosperity of the trading routes was important for the Mongols because it was a source of taxes.

Spread of Technology

As usual, with the exchange of culture and ideas comes a technological exchange. As the famous explorer Marco Polo noted in the 13th century, many regions in Asia, especially China, were populated by highly advanced civilizations for their time. In fact, many of the things he wrote about and reported back in Europe were met with great skepticism.

Thanks to the Silk Road, however, a lot of the things he talked about made their way to Europe for all to see. Among these things, there were numerous important technological breakthroughs achieved in China, which Europe would later heavily rely upon. Among these innovations were gunpowder, advanced paper making, and many other things that we now take as normal. While the Mongols themselves didn't exactly invent many of the things that Europe got thanks to the Silk Road, they undoubtedly made it possible for these crucial exchanges to take place. In fact, in many instances, these exchanges altered the course of human history.

Science and Globalization

Overall, the majority of inventions and scientific breakthroughs that the Europeans adopted from China made their way there via the Silk Road. In a way, making these transfers possible was just as important as the invention of this technology. New scientific breakthroughs wouldn't have been of much use to the world if they were limited to isolated societies in East Asia.

However, the Mongols didn't just build the Silk Road and go about their way. Instead, they made sure they got much more from this trade than just taxes. Because of the vastness of their empire, the Mongols had access to knowledge from distant parts of the world such as India, Persia, and the Middle East. All of these regions were home to great civilizations that had much to offer. Particularly important was the transfer of medical innovation and knowledge, and the Mongols dedicated themselves to studying Western medicine in depth, particularly under Kublai Khan.

This system of far-reaching trade and back and forth exchange was really an early form of free trade and globalization. These things are now an integral part of the human experience with many free trade agreements and economic unions, but it was the Mongol Empire and its Silk Road that pioneered the idea.

One Belt, One Road, Chinese strategic investment in the 21st century map

Spread of Firearms

The Mongols were quick to adopt many Chinese inventions that proved crucial in warfare, particularly gunpowder. One of the most prominent weapons that the Mongols used was the contemporary equivalent of grenades. These explosive devices struck fear into the enemy and made the Mongols a force to be reckoned with, especially during sieges.

Over time, such tactics made their way to Europe, and the Europeans were quick to pick up on the potential of gunpowder. Of course, this tactic had a major impact on the subsequent development of firearms, which brought an end to the days of knighthood and ushered in a whole new era in warfare. Eventually, the Europeans would conquer the world thanks to firearms, often subduing entire civilizations in the New World with little more than a few hundred men at arms. Over time, the innovations in this weaponry brought about the emergence of things like artillery and changed the concept of war forever.

Russia

As students of history know, Russia is still an indomitable country that has never been successfully conquered, except once. Indeed, the early days of Russian statehood saw many invasions and conquests by the Mongols who eventually held most of Russia in subjugation.

Ironically, some historians argue the Mongolian conquests led to the formation of Russia that we know today. The numerous Russian states at the time, such as Kievan Rus, Moscow, and others, were eventually forced to unite in order to push back and force the Mongols out of their lands. Separated by political leadership, language connected the Russian people, and in 1480, they managed to unite and defeat the Golden Horde. Eventually, the Russians would push further into Mongol-held areas, expanding their territories and finally building their own empire in the 18th century.

Other Military Inventions

Mongolian nomad

As you have learned, the Mongols were big on horse archery and, as such, they made some very important contributions and improvements to this art of war. One example was the Mongolian composite bow, which was vastly superior to the bows used in many other regions. As opposed to traditional, single-piece bows, composite bows were complex devices comprised of parts. Mongolian bows were vastly superior when it came to range, accuracy, and sheer power. They used horns, wood, sinew, and other materials to make their bows very durable and effective.

The Mongols also vastly improved one crucial aspect of horsemanship: the stirrup. As you may or may not know already, stirrups are footrests that greatly improve a rider's ability to control their horse and remain securely in the saddle. The stirrup has been around for a while, but the Mongols might have been the first people to use highly advanced metal stirrups over eleven centuries ago. The Mongols were able to stay glued to their horses in the heat of battle no matter what, often riding at great speeds and engaging enemies with their bows at the same time.

Riding stirrup

Dried Milk

Being a highly mobile, nomadic military force, the Mongols had to rely on durable and highly portable sources of nutrition that could keep them going in the field. One such innovation was dried milk, a quite common and accessible product nowadays.

Namely, the Mongols figured out that they could use the leftover curds after processing their milk into butter and cheese instead of just throwing it away. The Mongols would then dry out these bits and pieces, usually in the sun, and grind them down into powder. This primitive powder milk could be stored for cold winter months or taken on expeditions. All that the Mongols had to do was bring the milk back into liquid form with a bit of warm water. Of course, this potion was far from fresh milk, but it provided sustenance and, above all, convenience.

Support for Art

Being a warlike people that preferred the nomadic lifestyle well into their imperial stage, the Mongols weren't big on writing or producing fine art. In an interesting twist, however, they were admirers who had respect for art. Even though those who resisted their rule were squashed mercilessly, the Mongols would allow and support the artistic expression of the people they came in contact with.

During peaceful times, the Mongols were sort of like patrons for those local artists who impressed them. The Mongols thus protected and encouraged the art they liked under most of the Khans. Seeing as their empire stretched so far and wide, the Mongols came into contact with all sorts of artists in the Middle East, parts of India, elsewhere in Asia, and other locales. Over time, they also started to commission those artists to bring the Mongols' own designs to life in architecture, stonework, textile, and other fine crafts. In a way, the Mongols outsourced these jobs to those whom they perceived as skilled.

Postal System

An empire as vast as that of the Mongols needs a way for information to flow quickly and efficiently, and the Mongols were well aware of this. This was why they built something called the Yam route. The Yam was essentially a messenger system or a primitive form of postal service, and it stretched across important Mongolian lands.

Genghis Khan was the first to pay special attention to this system, expanding it to new lengths and making it perhaps the most efficient such system in the world. The Yam was basically a string of relay stations and resting stops that provided shelter, vital supplies, horses, and other necessities for messengers. The system was constantly buzzing with activity and it provided the intelligence backbone of the Mongol armies. Well-trained messengers could cover more than 150 miles each day using the Yam. Being such an important system, the Yam was maintained by the Russians well after the Mongols were forced out of their lands.

Chapter 7: What the Mongolian Empire Consisted of

One element adding to the frustrating success of the conquests of the Mongolians was the expert use of spies and propaganda. Before assaulting other peoples and societies, they generally requested for voluntary surrender and offered them to agree to peace. Just in case that this was accepted, the population was spared, and they were allowed to continue to live. If, though, resistance needed to be conquered, wholesale massacre or at the very least enslavement inevitably resulted, sparing only individuals whose unique abilities or capabilities were seen as beneficial. When it pertains to voluntary surrender, tribesmen or warriors were typically integrated into the Mongol forces and dealt with as federates. Personal commitment of federate rulers to the Mongol khan played a great part in all of this, as usually no official treaties were concluded. The "Mongol" armies, because of this, usually included only a minority of ethnic Mongols. The Mongols had a vast empire for a longer time period, and they are definitely worth the time researching. Their empire extended all the from East Asia to Europe and beyond, and to find how this came to be, is a topic that's fascinating to me. I hope you will find it interesting as well, as you study this brief book about the Mongol Empire.

Company of Genghis Khan's empire

At the time of the early phases of Mongol supremacy, the empire developed by Genghis soaked up societies in which a strong, merged, and efficient state power had developed. The social company of the Mongols was, though, identified by pastoralism and a decentralized patrilineal system of clans. Antagonism existed between a civilization of this nature and the ruled over sophisticated civilizations, between a reasonably little number of foreign conquerors and a numerically strong dominated population. In the early stages of conquest, the Mongols generally tried to enforce the social structure of the steppes on their new subjects. It was traditional for the Mongols to oppress a dominated people and to present entire communities to prominent army leaders as a sort of personal appanage. Those servants ended up being eventually an essential part of the dominating people. In the dominated parts a comparable process was adopted. Groups of the settled population, generally those living in a specific terrain, ended up being the personal effects of Mongol army leaders who abused the regional financial forces as they liked. No use was made from the existing state equipment or administration, and the previous political departments were completely overlooked. Nor was there an effort to balance out and organize all the many regional Mongol leaders who delighted in a high degree of independence from the court of the khans. Callous exploitation under strong army pressure was for that reason particular of the early stage of Mongol dominance, which might be said to have lasted till about 1234, some 7 years after Genghis Khan's death.

Genghis Khan

The main power rested with the khan, who was helped by army and political councilors. No department administration was, though, developed at the time of the early phases of

Genghis Khan's empire. The highly hierarchized army company of the Mongols had no political or administrative equivalent. The impact of the councilors, who were selected by the khan no matter their citizenship, was nonetheless great. It was a previous Jin topic, the Khitan Yelü Chucai (1190-- 1244), a guy of high skills with an outstanding Chinese education, who discouraged Genghis from transforming the entirety of north China into pastureland. Other councilors were Uyghurs, and for a little time the Uyghur language was as much used in the court chancery as Mongol. The Uyghur script was also adopted for writing Mongol. The oldest recognized file in the Mongol language is a stone engraving sculpted in around the year 1224.

The economy of the dominated parts wasn't appropriately organized throughout the period of conquest. The abolition of highly organized federal governments gave a chance for the exploitation of regional production by the Mongol appanage-holders who relied to a great degree on non-Mongol tax-farmers. There was no single monetary system for the entire empire or perhaps for big parts of it. The lack of civil company at the top, the great independence of the different appanages, and the high top priority accorded to army affairs had a highly breaking down impact and were, at the very least in the early stages of Mongol reign, harmful to financial development and success. The Mongol empire was, under Genghis and his followers, not yet a state in the typical sense of the word but a large heap of commonly different areas held together by army dominance.

As the empire grew through new conquests after Genghis's death, the exact same pattern repeated itself: a period of army, and at the exact same time decentralized, the reign marked the first stage of Mongol supremacy. The outcome was a visible version of practice within the empire. Recently dominated parts were still subject to direct exploitation bearing the imprint of a nomadic and army mindset, but, in those parts which had been ruled over earlier, efforts were made to develop a state equipment and administration to combine Mongol reign. This was done primarily in agreement with the standard administrative system of the individual terrain.

This general propensity, with the lack of an initial Mongol principle for ruling a settled population, represent the totally different development that happened in different nations. That led to an empire that could not have been "Mongol" but was a Chinese, Persian, or main Asian empire with a Mongol dynasty. This pattern was uttered more in some places than others because the absorptive power of the different societies varied in strength. In China, for example, the Mongols could preserve their reign better than in other places because the strong Chinese custom of central state power provided a steady structure of governmental company.

The original lack of a state principle on the part of the Mongols is shown in the judgment clan's mindset to the empire. The empire was considered to be not the khan's personal effects but the treasure of the royal clan as a whole. Already in Genghis's life time the empire was split amongst his 4 preferred sons into ulus, a Mongol word which represents the supremacy over a particular number of tribe instead of a plainly specified terrain. Tolui, the youngest, got the eastern part-- the original homeland of the Mongols together with the adjacent parts of north China. Ögödei ended up being ruler of the western part of the steppes (modern-day northern Xinjiang and western Mongolia). Chagatai got the territories of Khara-Khitai (modern-day northern Iran and southern Xinjiang). The oldest child, Jöchi, followed by his child Batu, ruled over southwest Siberia and west Turkistan (a region later referred to as the terrain of the Golden Crowd). To these 4 Mongol empires a fifth was added when Hülegü, a child of Tolui, finished the conquest of Iran, Iraq, and Syria and ended up being the creator of the Il-Khanid dynasty in Iran. The unity of the Mongol empire was for this reason from start weakened by breaking down aspects, and the history of the empire after Genghis's death could as a result be partitioned into 2 periods, the first being identified by relative unity in the empire governed by a great khan who was acknowledged by all branches of the noble clan, the 2nd demonstrating a basically complete independence of the separate empires, which afterwards had no typical history.

Chapter 8: The Structure of the Empire

At the time of the early stages of Mongol rule, Genghis Khan's kingdom soaked up societies that had formed a strong, joined, and efficient state authority. The Mongols' social order, on the other hand, was represented by pastoralism and a decentralized patrilineal clan system. Antagonism developed between such a civilization and the caught innovative civilizations, and between a little number of foreign conquerors and a very big conquered people. At the time of the early phases of conquest, the Mongols tried to enforce the steppes' social structure on their new people. The Mongols were well-known for oppressing dominated tribe and presenting whole communities to popular army leaders as a type of personal appanage. Servants formed an inseparable part of the dominating people eventually. A comparable strategy was used in the dominated parts. Mongol army chiefs made groups of the settled people, normally those living in a particular province, their personal effects, using the regional financial forces as they pleased. The existing state equipment and administration were entirely neglected, as were the prior political distinctions. Likewise, there wasn't any effort to organize the many regional Mongol leaders who were fairly independent of the khans' court. The early stage of Mongol supremacy, which can be considered to have lasted till around the year 1234, some 7 years after Genghis Khan's death, was defined by callous exploitation under strong army pressure.

The khan, who was helped by army and political councilors, held main power. Throughout the early stages of Genghis Khan's kingdom, though, no department administration was developed. The Mongols' incredibly hierarchical army structure did not have a political or administrative equivalent. The councilors, who were designated by the khan despite of their citizenship, wielded substantial power. Genghis was discouraged from changing all of north China into pastureland by a previous Jin topic, the Khitan Yelü Chucai (1190--1244), a guy of exceptional qualities with a great Chinese education. Other councilors were Uyghurs, and the Uyghur language was used in the court chancery as thoroughly as Mongol for a while. Mongols were also written in the Uyghur script. A stone engraving sculpted in the year 1224 is the first recognized record in the Mongol language.

At the time of the conquest, the caught parts' economies were not well grouped and led. The removal of well organized supervisions provided a chance for Mongol appanage-holders, who relied greatly on non-Mongol tax-farmers, to make use of regional output. For the whole empire, or perhaps for significant areas of it, there was no unified monetary system. The absence of civil structure at the top, the huge independence of the many appanages, and the high value given to army activities had a deeply destabilizing effect and were damaging to financial improvement and success, at the very least in the early periods of Mongol reign. Under Genghis and his followers, the Mongol empire wasn't yet a state in the conventional sense, but rather a big assemblage of diverse areas kept together by army may.

After Genghis' death, the empire broadened through added conquests, and the exact same pattern emerged: a period of army and decentralized reign described the initial stage of Mongol supremacy. As a consequence, there was a substantial distinction in practice across the empire. Recently caught parts were still subjected to direct exploitation with the imprint of a nomadic and army mindset, but attempts were made to develop a state equipment and administration in parts that had already been ruled over so as to combine Mongol power. That was generally done in agreement with the particular terrain's historical administrative system.

This general pattern, in addition to the absence of an initial Mongol model for ruling a settled population, clarifies why unique nations developed in such diverse ways. That led to a Chinese, Persian, or Main Asian empire with a Mongol dynasty, instead of a "Mongol" empire. Since the absorptive strength of the numerous societies differed in strength, this pattern was more noticeable in some spots than others. The Mongols, for instance, had the ability to keep their authority in China better than in other places just because of the strong Chinese custom of central state power, which provided a steady governmental structure.

The Mongols' early absence of a state concept is reflected in the judgment clan's mindset towards the empire. The empire was viewed as the treasure of the royal family tree as an entire, instead of the khan's personal possession. The empire was split amongst Genghis' 4 preferred sons into ulus, a Mongol word that represents supremacy over a group of tribe instead of a plainly specified area, even at the time of his life time. Tolui, the youngest, was given the eastern half, that included the Mongols' native nation and parts of north China. Gödei rose to the throne of the western steppes (modern-day northern Xinjiang and western Mongolia). Chagatai was given the Khara-Khitai areas (modern-day northern Iran and southern Xinjiang). Jöchi, the oldest child, ruled over southwest Siberia and west Turkistan, followed by his child Batu (a region later called the terrain of the Golden Crowd). Hülegü, a child of Tolui, finished the conquest of Iran, Iraq, and Syria and established the Il-Khanid dynasty in Iran, bringing the overall number of Mongol empires to 5. The Mongol empire's unity was therefore weakened from the start by breaking down aspects, and the empire's history after Genghis' death can hence be separated into 2 periods, the first identified by relative unity in the empire governed by a great khan acknowledged by all branches of the noble clan, and the 2nd identified by more or less complete independence of the separate empires, which afterwards had no typical history.

Chapter 9: Union in the Empire

Not much later, after Genghis Khan's death, a kuriltai (at times written kurultai; "universal assembly") of Mongol nobles was contacted us to choose the new great khan in harmony with custom. Jöchi, the oldest of Genghis' successors, had passed away 6 months before his dad, and the Mongols usually followed the law of primogeniture. The oldest enduring child, Chagatai, was passed over, and gödei was ultimately called great khan (1229-- 41). He led his projects from Karakorum, which is situated on the Orhon River in main Mongolia. Chinkai, a Kereit Nestorian Christian, acted as head of chancery, while Yelü Chucai stayed his senior counsel. In modern texts, gödei is illustrated as a man of severe mood, industrious but vulnerable to enjoyment, and a huge drinker. His wars, like his dad's, were run simultaneously by independent generals in the field, but they were always led by orders from the khan himself, which were sent out by means of a messenger system that covered practically all of Asia.

A war was carried out in east Asia against the residues of the Juchen Jin empire in northern China. Because he was assaulted from both sides, the Jin emperor found himself in a desperate circumstance. The Jin had caught north China from the Tune in the prior century, but the Tune had later on joined with the Mongols. The Jin capital of Kaifeng caught a combined Mongol-Chinese assault in the year 1234, and Aizong, the last Jin emperor, committed himself.

Westward projects

New explorations against the west were carried out in the year 1236, seemingly with the objective of ruling over Russia and even eastern Europe and including them to Batu Khan's ulus. The Volga Bulgars' empire was damaged in 1237/38, leading the way for Russia appropriate to emerge. At the period, main and northern Russia was made up of city-states and independent princedoms that succumbed to the Mongol forces' furious attack one by one. The Mongol push towards the Baltic Sea was only stopped by the Russian winter season; Novgorod, a rich mall, was therefore one of the few Russian towns to leave sacking. After the collapse of Kyiv, Russia's resistance came to an end (December 1240). More raids were launched against Poland, Galicia, and Volhynia, with advance groups reaching Breslaù (Wrocaw) in Silesia. Regardless of a disastrous defeat near Legnica (on April 9th, in 1241) by a combined force of German and Polish knights led by Duke Henry II of Silesia, the Mongols decided not to advance further into main Germany. Rather, they headed south to join forces with their fighters stationed in Hungary.

King Béla IV wasn't shocked by the attack on Hungary. The Kipchaks, a Turkic wanderer population in southern Russia, had undergone Mongol dominance, but under their chieftain Kuten, a great deal of them left to Hungary, where they were secured by the Hungarians, from the Don and Dnieper steppes. Batu said the Kipchaks were his vassals and asked for that the King of Hungary return them to Russia, threatening to fight Hungary if his demand wasn't satisfied. He dispatched his southern force on Hungary after getting no reaction.

In April in the year 1241, this army, led by Subutai, a capable leader, beat the Hungarians at Mohi. Béla IV, King of Hungary, was forced to run away to Croatia. The Mongols don't appear to have ever meant to settle completely in Silesia and Moravia. They did, though, establish a nucleus of Mongol governance in Hungary, and even produced coins, some of which have made it through. Just because of their resemblances to the meadows of southern Russia, where the Mongols developed themselves completely, the Hungarian plains could have attracted them as appropriate pasturelands (as the later Golden Crowd).

Mongol soldiers had also been active in Iran, Georgia, and Greater Armenia in the preceding years. The Khwrezm sultan, who got away before Genghis Khan's intrusions, ended up being emperor of a kingdom in northwest Iran and tried fruitless to fend off the Mongols. In the year 1231, he was assassinated. In the year 1236, Georgia was pushed to acknowledge Mongol reign. The death of the great khan gödei, though, stopped the Mongol development in Europe and the Near East (this happened on December 11th, in 1241). Some of Genghis' descendants changed their strategies just because they needed to be present at the kuriltai, which needed to chose an heir, and they needed to assert their claims. Batu and his generals gave up all of their eastern European holdings. The year 1241 therefore marks a watershed moment in European history, because Hungary, at least, would've been a Mongol rule had it not been for the unforeseen death of gödei.

The appointment of a new khan leader

Just because no agreement could be reached, the election of a new great khan showed difficult. In the interim, Töregene, Gödei's widow, ruled with the Mongol nobles' assent (1242-- 46). Her ask for Güyük's appointment was consulted with intense opposition from Batu, who actually believed he had a more powerful claim as a grand son of Genghis's oldest child. In the year 1246, she achieved success in protecting Güyük's election. Giovanni da Pian del Carpini, who happened to be in Karakorum at the time as papal envoy, wrote an eyewitness description of the election. Güyük was a greatly different individual from his foe Batu. He was motivated by Nestorianism and chosen Christian consultants, though Batu still practiced conventional Mongol shamanism and was unconcerned about any other faith. The 2 competitors started planning a fight, but Güyük's unfortunate death (1248) put an end to both the familial competition with Batu and the possibility of a Mongol court controlled by Christian impact.

The empire was given to Güyük's widow, Ogul-Gaimish, who ruled as regent for 3 years till the nobility had the ability to strike an accord. Batu himself revealed some interest in presuming the outright power of great khan, but because of his innovative age, he ultimately forfeited and convinced the Mongol nobility to elect Möngke Khan, child of Tolui. That meant that the empire's overlordship moved from the family of gödei to the descendants of Genghis's youngest child. After Möngke's election (1251), the Chagatai branch of the family felt betrayed, and violent competition emerged between the 2 homes.

Möngke's rule was just one of the most remarkable in history.

Möngke had acquired prestige and distinguished himself in the field throughout Batu's western explorations. He was a very good king who carried on Güyük's policy of universal tolerance for all faiths. Throughout his reign, the capital of Karakorum accomplished a level of elegance that showed the empire's size. The French friar Willem van Ruysbroeck, a European visitor to the palace in the month of January in 1254, gave an interesting account of the Mongol city, where Christian churches, Muslim mosques, and Buddhist temples grew and envoys from all over the world assembled. Möngke went on to broaden his kingdom at the exact same time, getting ready for the conquest of formerly unconquered nearby nations. His 2 brothers, Hülegü and Kublai, helped him in this undertaking. He committed the fight against Iran to Hülegü, of which only one province in the north had fallen under Mongol control. Hülegü started his attack in the year 1255. In 1256, he beat the powerful Assassin sect's resistance and continued to Iraq. Baghdad, the caliphate's capital, was caught by the Mongols in the year 1258, and the last Abbasid caliph was executed. The spiritual circumstance in the Near East was exceptionally impacted by these events. Christians and Shias invited the Mongols because the caliphate's Sunni orthodoxy had alienated them. Christians in Syria, Palestine, and Asia

Minor hoped that Hülegü, who was considered as a protector against their Islamic rulers and whose partner was a Nestorian Christian, would make added advances. Hülegü's army attacked Syria in 1259, catching Damascus and Aleppo on their way to the Mediterranean Sea. The way to Egypt seemed open, but the Mamluk army squashed the Mongols at the Battle of Ayn Jlt in the year 1260. Egypt was saved, and the Mongol empire's more growth was stopped.

Kublai's Election.

On the other side of Asia, a project against China was also effective. Kublai was the leader, and his generals outflanked the Chinese strongholds by marching to Annam through the southwest of China, which was controlled by the self-governing Tai kingdom of Nan-chao. Möngke later on presumed command of the China project (1257). Once again, fate stepped in and brought Mongol operations to a stop, as it had done in the year 1241. Möngke died in the field at the siege of a provincial town in Sichuan in the month of August 1259. As is popular, an internal fight appeared between many competitors to the title of great khan. While still in the field (1260), Kublai won his own election, but his more youthful brother Arigböge announced himself Khan of Karakorum. Hülegü was too far, and fascinated in his Syrian project, to have any effect on the election. He appears to have chosen Kublai, and the 2 brothers stayed friendly, regardless of (or maybe simply because) Kublai's domain being so far and his overlordship more or less small.

In any case, Kublai's climb to the throne marks a watershed moment in the Mongol empires' history. In concept, as great khan, Kublai was the ruler of an empire that stretched from China and Korea to Iran and southern Russia, but the variety of the dominated nations ended up being progressively evident. Kublai grew to see himself more as a Chinese emperor than anything else, and the other rules did the same, developing along less and less Mongol lines. This pattern could be connected to the numerous khans' conversion to other religious beliefs, especially Islam and Buddhism. The move of Kublai's capital to Beijing (1260), which he started to restore in the year 1267, highlighted his shift from Mongol to Chinese civilisation. Mongolia, and even Kublai's rules, were no longer the true heart of the empire.

Chapter 10: China's Yuan Dynasty

Kublai Khan was just one of China's most effective rulers. By ruining the country Tune empire, he had the ability to unify the nation (1279). He dealt with the deposed royal family with respect and prohibited his generals from turning to indiscriminate massacre, in contrast to former practice. The Mongol-Chinese kingdom got no added terrain after 1279, and 2 attempts to push Mongol power to Japan were foiled by the Kamikaze of 1274 and 1281. None of the ensuing Yuan emperors could match Kublai's stature. Temür (1295-- 1307), Genghis Khan's grand son, had the ability to keep Mongol reign undamaged and hold his position in the face of repeated efforts by the gödei branch of Genghis Khan's family. In 1301, the competing khan Kaidu was beat, and peace was brought back in the empire's northwestern areas.

Although small uprisings against the federal government could still be put down by Mongol forces, the court's power started to subside. Later emperors' power was harmed by bad blood and court intrigues. Some times, teenagers who were absolutely nothing more than puppets in the hands of enthusiastic ministers were enthroned. The emperors' death is mirrored in the pictures that have endured. Even though common Mongols stayed antagonistic to every little thing Chinese, the effect of Chinese civilization grew at court and amongst members of the Mongol elite. Togon-temür (ruled 1333-- 68), the last Mongol emperor, was only thirteen years of age when he ended up being emperor. He had acquired a fundamental Chinese education and, like some of his predecessors, was a ernest Buddhist and a kindhearted but weak king. At the time of the preliminary years of his reign, though, authority was in the hands of Bayan, an anti-Chinese minister whose actions irritated the bitterness of the informed Chinese against Mongol reign.

Mongol power in China is subsiding.

The last decrease of Mongol supremacy in China, and also the disorderly conditions that existed under Togon-reign, temür's were just a few of China's many "periods of trouble." There was significant discontentment, which often manifested itself as regional uprisings against the Mongol federal government. The premises for this development were mainly financial, and insurgents launched their attacks on the regional authorities in the countryside, as is traditional in China. The peasantry's circumstance was alarming in lots of ways; little farmers and renters needed to bear the impact of high tax and corvée charges. All Chinese people were infuriated by the Mongol aristocrats' and bureaucrats' arbitrariness.

The Mongol ruling class appears to have never ever had the ability to develop gratifying relations with China's agrarian population. The Mongol legislation on searching showed their absence of compassion for farming issues: peasants were prohibited to safeguard their crops from game animals and were also needed to join the Mongols in searching explorations, which undoubtedly triggered substantial damage in the fields. Mongol-Chinese relations were generally better in the cities than they were in the countryside. In 1351, when the federal government chose to execute a huge plan for water preservation in the Huang He (Yellow River) area, which had been devastated by extreme floods, the circumstance ended up being especially tense. Regional insurgent leaders were generally from the poorer classes of society. Salt smugglers, petty authorities, sectarian leaders, monks, and shamans were amongst them. Disobediences were specifically typical in the southeastern provinces, which were agriculturally the wealthiest and therefore the most mercilessly misused area of the empire. For ages, the province of Zhejiang had been the world's biggest rice surplus area, and Beijing, with its big population, had long counted on supplies from this area. The circumstance in the capital ended up being perilous when disobediences interrupted the paths of communication between north and south. The currency's fiat money ended up being totally useless, and the treasury was rapidly tired. This hindered the federal government's army exertions again.

It is a striking aspect of the history of these years that the many disobediences, which took place individually of each other in the beginning, were not influenced by nationalist belief amongst the oppressed peasants, but were directed against the higher classes despite of their ethnic culture. The Chinese upper class had just as much to fear from the insurgents as the Mongols, according to modern sources. That helps to comprehend why so many Chinese people went on to help the federal government. They appeared to prefer the severe rule of immigrants over their compatriots' violent populist movements. Those insurgents committed atrocities that functioned as a major obstacle to a more general rebellion for several years. Slowly, though, more informed Chinese were won over to the reason for the rebels, who in turn discovered how to handle administrative and army concerns from them.

Previous monk Zhu Chongba was the most effective rebel leader. He was born into a simple peasant family, but he beat his challengers in terms of energy, patience, and army expertise. He achieved success in not only developing himself in essential financial fields, but also in eliminating his challengers in the power battle. Zhu eventually drove the Mongols out of Beijing (1368) and developed the Ming dynasty as the new emperor. By 1359, he had chosen the rule name Hongwu and, with the help of experienced generals, had extended his rule over all of northern China. Even so, Mongol provincial leaders in the southwest withstood, and Ming reign didn't come to the southwest till much later (Szechwan, 1371; Yünnan, 1382). Togon-temür, the last Mongol emperor, pulled away to the steppes and passed away there in 1370.

The Mongols' defeat cannot, though, be credited to degeneracy or corruption by the relaxing effects of life in an extremely civilized Chinese environment. Following events, it was clear that the Mongols had not lost their army passion, and they stayed a danger to the northwest Chinese frontier. Because of this potential risk, the Hongwu emperor might have chosen to build his capital not in Beijing, which was more or less a frontier town, but in Nanjing, where he had formerly set up his home in 1364. With Zhu Chongba's ascension to royal power and the re-establishment of Chinese federal government, not only the Mongols, but also the many non-Mongol immigrants who had held office or made fortunes as merchants under the Mongols, political and financial activities stopped. Those individuals who chose to remain in China changed their last names and grew more incorporated in time. Foreign religious beliefs like Islam and Christendom have been removed of their opportunities. Because of the Chinese's strong nationalist emotions, Christendom was efficiently removed.

Mongol supremacy has had some impacts.

It's unrealistic to determine the general impact of Mongol supremacy over China. The suspension of literary evaluations, the exemption of Chinese from higher positions, and the taking place disappointment of the old gentility of scholar-officials led to an intellectual eremitism. A class that was prohibited from taking part in political matters went on to practice conventional customs of Chinese literature and art. The only departments of the civil service where informed Chinese partnership was definitely needed were those handling routine and historiography. The Mongol language never ever entirely changed Chinese as a medium for historiography or main files, and many Mongol engravings are multilingual. Possibly simply because the ruling minority was unenthusiastic in, or maybe not able to read, what their subjects wrote in Chinese, Chinese literary life stayed extremely open. After the year 1280, Chinese authors had the ability to easily show their patriotic, loyalist, and anti-Mongol beliefs.

In the sphere of literature, the period of Mongol rule over China is also marked by a considerable output of play and well-known books produced in the vernacular. Nevertheless, this practice is unassociated to Mongol rule simply because it is challenging to imagine a Mongol audience in front of a Chinese stage. A sociological element, the merchant class's broadening power and prominence, could have had a vital role. Traders and merchants was among the few sectors of the population who took advantage of Mongol control. Priests of non-Chinese religious beliefs (Islam, Christianity, and Judaism) were another group that took advantage of the tax exemption granted to Buddhist and, to a lower level, Daoist clergy in China. At the very least at court, the

Mongols deserted their old forms of religious belief and ended up being mostly converts to Tibetan Buddhism, which was already thriving in China under Kublai Khan. The increasing number of Mongols given Buddhist names stemmed from Tibetan shows Tibetan Buddhism's broadening appeal. On the other side, Chinese Buddhism stayed mainly opposed to Tibetan clergy, who were hated not only for their religious belief but also for being a preferred fan of the intruders. Most Buddhist abbeys in China were also fortress of Chinese conventional culture. Daoism is the exact same way. Regardless of the fact that Daoist clergy were initially granted the exact same opportunities as Buddhist clergy, the Daoist religious belief had already started to face main oppression under Kublai, maybe just because Buddhist clergy saw Daoism as a hazardous competitor and Daoist sects and abbeys were seen, not without reason, as hotbeds of secret activities and unchecked nationalism.

All things considered, it is safe to say that Mongol rule had really little effect on Chinese society as a whole. Nonetheless, in terms of law and federal government, it was accountable for a particular departure from developed moral requirements of conduct. The fact that China had been under barbarian reign for more than a century could have added to the Ming dynasty's autocratic and totalitarian qualities.

The Mongols, as an entire, were fairly unenthusiastic in Chinese culture. Nonetheless, certain them ended up being accomplished Chinese intellectuals, and their poesy and calligraphy were on par with regional Chinese. After some preliminary exertions under Kublai, the prospering emperors motivated translations from Chinese into Mongol, and the first specimens of Mongol printing were made in China. Most of these translations have since been ruined as a result of Ming nationalism, but the few making it through residues, specifically Buddhist works, are important to the history of the Mongol language. In or soon after 1368, the Mongols were ousted from China. They resided in Mongolia for the next 2 centuries precisely as they had before their conquests: as an aggressive wanderer individuals with hardly several residues of their long vacation amongst the Chinese.

The Mongols' later history

The Mongols were limited to their ancestral terrain in the steppes for some centuries after 1368, but the memory of their previous splendour and supremacy over China triggered regular efforts to recover their lost position. Yet, the Ming emperors considered the Mongols to be their subjects and Mongolia to be a part of their world. In addition to the routine fights between contending clans, the Mongols' history in these years is controlled by their interactions with China. The early Ming emperors tried to take Mongolia's plains some times, but without enduring success. In 1388, Toquz Temür, Togon-grandson, temür's was beat by a Chinese expeditionary force near Lake Buir in northeastern Mongolia. Another Chinese exploration reached the Onon River a century later, in 1410, and beat Oljai Temür (ruled 1403--12). Oljai's authority was ultimately taken over by the Oirat clan. When Esen Taiji (ruled 1439-- 55) launched a fight against the Ming empire in the mid-15th century, the Oirats' strength reached its peak (1449). Esen achieved success in recording Ming Emperor Zhengtong and transferring him to Mongolia as a detainee of war. He even attacked Beijing, but the Chinese fort's solid resistance, in addition to instability in the Mongol camp and deft Chinese diplomacy, triggered the tide to move.

Chapter 11: The Empires in Central Asia

The ulus consisting of the old Khara-Khitai empire reaching east of Lake Balkhash, and that includes the whole Tarim Basin, and Transoxania and Afghanistan, had been given to Genghis Khan's Chagatai clan. Their empire had a mainly Turkic population, and steppe customs stayed substantially more powerful there than in China's existing Mongol rule. The Muslim sanctuary occupants' society had only a little effect on the Chagatai empire's nomadic nature, and the empire's expansionist goals acquired from prior kings were continuously felt. Because there are few trustworthy records, the history of the Chagatai empire seems a bit muddled; even the khans' rule dates aren't always sturdy. The Chagatai empire was governed by gödei's descendant Kaidu from 1267 to 1301, and it was only after the latter's death that the Chagatai khans restored their independence.

The Chagatai dynasty was well-known for its repeated efforts to catch India through Afghanistan and the Punjab Plain in diplomacy.

The intrusion of India was just one of Genghis' original objectives, but it was rapidly deserted in favor of other fights. The Chagatai kings sent out forces into India through Afghanistan on some times, primarily because fairly steady federal governments on all other frontiers-- the Yüan empire in the east and the Il-Khan state in the west-- stopped an aggressive position. As a consequence, the only feasible attack direction was to the south. The Mongols stayed a very serious adversary for the Muslim sultans of Delhi for decades. Under Duwa Khan (1301-- 05), the Mongol intrusions from Afghanistan were exceptionally relentless, and the Delhi ruler Al al-Dn Khalj was only able to hold his capital against the Chagatai expeditionary forces with great trouble.

In spite of the conversion of earlier khans, Islam's condition had stayed vulnerable. When the khan Tarmashirin re-adopted Islam (1326) following a quick period of internal peace (1301-- 25), there was a short-term divide between the eastern and western halves of his world. According to some variations, Tarmashirin was murdered by

Buddhist and shamanic followers because of his conversion to Islam. The empire was reunified under Tughluq Temür (1347-- 63), but his followers were only puppets. The real power was in the hands of the amir Timur (Tamerlane, 1336--1405), who extended the Chagatai dynasty in spite of not being a Mongol. At the time of the 14th century, the impact of Chagatai Turkish grew substantially, while Mongol was still employed as a main language in the Turfan area as late as 1369. The Chagatai ulus, on the other hand, had virtually stopped to be a Mongol empire and had become a Chagatai and Islamic kingdom under Timur's reign. Nevertheless, vestiges of Mongol control might still be seen in Afghanistan; the Moghol people speak a Mongol dialect with some antiquated characteristics that goes back to the Mongol conquest in the 13th century. Persian replaced Mongol and, to a lower degree, Chagatai Turkish as the authority and literary languages.

The Shaybnid dynasty was another nation that, regardless of being governed by Genghis Khan's descendants, should be considered basically Chagatai. Shaybn, a grand son of Genghis and a boy of Juchi, ruled over the properties east and southeast of the Ural Mountains. Ab'l-Khayr (ruled 1428-- 68) was just one of his forefathers who ended up being emperor of the Uzbeks. Muammad Shaybn, his grand son, dominated Bukhara and Hert from the Timurids, and his followers ruled in Bukhara till 1599. Parts of Transcaspia were governed by other branches of the exact same dynasty, like the Nogay and Astrakhan khans. Only insofar as their sultans were patrilineal descendants of Genghis Khan were these worlds considered Mongol. They didn't have any Mongol qualities at all. Their society was Islamic with a substantial infusion of Persian affects, and their language was Chagatai Turkish. The Shaybnids controlled the khanate of Khiva from 1512, and its last khan, Abd Allh, was gotten rid of by the Soviet federal government in 1920, regardless of the fact that Russian supremacy had already been developed over the whole area in the 1860s and 1870s.

Chapter 12: In Iran, the Il-Khans

As a result of the Mongol queens' spiritual leaning in Iran, the ulus of Hülegü were put in an uncommon political situation from the start. Hülegü's anti-Islamic position and attack on the caliphate triggered a schism with the Golden Crowd in southern Russia, where Berke, Batu's brother, had converted to Islam. The Il-Khans ("local khans") of Iran, on the other hand, at first stayed devoted fans of China's great khan Kublai, while Berke backed the impostor Arigböge who rose against Kublai. Hülegü stayed hostile to Egypt, the most effective Islamic force in the Near East, thus Berke's alliance with the Mamluks in Egypt, which was checked in the year 1261, came practically naturally. A Mongol ruler aligned himself with a foreign power against another Mongol for the first time in history. This political constellation included European powers too. The pope and the kings of France provided security to the Crusader-founded Christian republics of Tripoli and Acre. It's not unexpected, then, that the Il-Khans were viewed as potential allies against Islamic Egypt in Rome and Paris.

In the year 1265, Hülegü's child Abagha prospered his dad. Abagha's spouse was a Byzantine, the daughter of Emperor Michael VIII Palaeologus, and he tried to reinforce political and army relate to the Holy See, England, and France through the Nestorian patriarchs, whom he highly preferred. His repeated efforts to catch Syria and Egypt, on the other hand, were a definite failure, as he was not able to work with Byzantium or the Christian countries. Abagha passed away in the year 1282, and the liberal policy towards Christians was supported under Arghn (1284-- 91), who was himself a Buddhist. He, too, preferred the Nestorians, sending out the Nestorian ecclesiastic Rabban bar Sauma to Europe as his ambassador to create much deeper ties with the Christian countries. Bar Sauma headed to Byzantium first, then to Paris, where he met Philip the Fair (1287). He met King Edward I of England in Bordeaux, and Pope Nicholas IV gave him an audience in Rome (1288). Yet, no concrete results followed. The taking place letters of Arghn to Philip of France (1289) and Pope Nicholas IV (1290) are linguistic and historic treasures.

Arghn relied greatly on the Jewish doctor Miserable al-Dawlah, who was designated inspector general of the treasury in the year 1288, in internal affairs. Right after, anti-Sad resistance developed, triggering anti-Jewish rioting. When Arghn's inheritor Gaykhatu (1291-- 95) introduced paper currency based upon the Chinese model, the empire's monetary condition ended up being a lot more treacherous. That paper currency was a devastating catastrophe, leading to complete financial mayhem.

Mamud Ghzn's reign (1295-- 1304) saw substantial developments in some parts. He set up financial and financial reforms and reorganized the empire's federal government. His conversion to Islam is a substantial pivotal moment in Mongol and Iranian history. Buddhists were maltreated as idolaters, and Jews and Christians were amongst those that suffered. The Mongols' conversion to Islam helped the assimilation of Mongols and Turks in north Iran by getting rid of spiritual barriers. Ghzn also announced himself totally independent of the Beijing court, and all referrals to the great khans were removed from currency engravings and main documents. To stress his sovereignty, he changed his name from Il-Khan to khan. The death in the year 1294 of Kublai Khan, whose connections with his nephews and great-nephews in Iran had always been friendly, might have set off the facility of Iran as an independent kingdom.

Ghzn's brother, Ijeitü (1304-- 16), became a successor of him as khan after his unforeseen death at the age of 31 (1304). He was born Nicholas and was baptized as a Christian, but later converted to Islam. He followed Ghzn's reform method and kept his advisors, and that includes statesman and chronicler Rashd al-Dn. The Il-Khans' prior capital was Tabriz, but Ijeitü transferred his home to Solniyyeh near Qazvn (1307). In regards to diplomacy, the new khan chose to resume engagement with European countries, as had his predecessors. His letter to Philip IV of France in 1307, in which he offered to maintain friendly relations, has made it through. Ghzn and Ijeitü were both popular advocates of the arts and literature. The absorption of the

Mongols by Iranian civilisation grew more popular under the impact of Islam. In spite of the fact that Ijeitü's letter to Philip was written in Mongol, he describes himself as sultan instead of khan and uses a Muslim date in addition to the standard Mongol categorization of years based upon the animal cycle. The seals are in Chinese, as are those on Arghn's letters. The Il-Khan empire's coexistence of Mongol, Turkic, Iranian, and Chinese aspects lasted over half a century, though Islamic and Iranian affects eventually shown to be the most effective.

In spite of this, Iran stayed under the impact of Chinese civilization for a very long time. Its 13th and 14th century mini paintings, especially those of the so-called Demotte Shh-nmeh, are obviously based upon Chinese customs. Under Mongol rule, Iran produced a chronicler who was probably the first to try to produce a real world history. That was Rashd al-Jmi Dn's al-tawrkh ("The Collection of Chronicles"), that included not only Mongol history but also Indian, Chinese, and European history (the Franks). Just in a location like Iran, where cultural and political relations with China,

European powers, and other Mongol empires existed together, could such universality be expected.

Ab Miserable, Ijeitü's child and successor, was the first Il-Khan king to have a Muslim name. Because he was only twelve years of age when he rose to the throne (1317), regional amirs wielded the majority of the power. inner strife and progressive collapse took place over the next twenty years. The Il-Khan kingdom successfully disappeared as a political union when Ab Miserable passed away childless in 1335.

Chapter 13: A Tumultuous Childhood

The name we all know this influential historical figure by is, of course, Genghis Khan. However, this namesake isn't actually a real name. Rather, it is a title which roughly translates to "universal ruler." The man who would come to be known as Genghis Khan was not born with this name, but he would certainly come to earn it. Instead, the mighty warlord known as Genghis Khan was born, simply, Temujin.

The name Temujin might not have the same perpetuity and might that Genghis Khan has, but the lineage associated with Temujin was not something to be scoffed at. Temujin's family history is rife with powerful reputation, at least on his father's side. He was born into the House of Borjigin. This clan made up the ruling class of the Mongolian population. Temujin's father, Yesugei, was a major player in Mongolian politics, and was descended from incredibly powerful names in the history of Mongolia. He was the grandson of Khabul Khan, and the nephew of Ambaghai and Hotula Khan as well. These three individuals were all prominent rulers of the

Khamag Mongol confederation, which was essentially a loose pact between Mongolian tribes that strived to retain peace and balance in the Mongolian region. Mongolia at this time was comprised of little more than nomadic tribes who had scant need for political constraints. It was the beginnings of political stability in the region, at least in some capacity, and Yesugei would carry on their legacy.

Temujin was also a direct ancestor of Bondochar Munkhag, a Mongolian warlord who, in all of Mongolian history, is only exceeded in reputation by Temujin himself. Bondochar Munkhag was the founder of the Borjigin clan, and had earned his place in Mongolian history as one of their greatest unifiers. He led the most significant Mongolian expansion endeavors in history, until, of course, Temujin came around. Clearly, it was in Temujin's blood to play an active role within the Mongolian Empire, but he of course exceeded all expectations.

Temujin's mother didn't come from a lineage nearly as notable as his father had. Hoelun was nothing more than a captive, and likely did not willingly give Yesugei the four sons he would have by her. She belonged to the Olkhunut tribe, a less prominent nomadic tribe that would still play a role later in Temujin's life.

This was a period of time and in a part of the world where men were the major players in society, and they called all of the shots. Women were more of a commodity, and property available to be traded and married off for nothing more than political gain. Women were used for various purposes, many of which were quite homely. They prepared meals and raised children, primarily, but they were also used to collect bows and arrows after a battle. Sometimes, in keeping with the warlike Mongolian spirit, women were also in charge of finishing off wounded enemies on the battlefield.

In Hoelun's case, she was originally meant to be married to a member of the Merkit confederation, a neighboring coalition of nomadic tribes. On her way to the Merkit camp, however, Yesugei and a band of soldiers attacked her caravan. Hoelun was kidnapped and taken back to Yesugei's encampment. Here, he proclaimed her as his chief wife, an ironically honorable title within Mongolian culture. Polygamy was not an uncommon occurrence amongst these tribes, but the chief wife enjoyed a higher privilege than any of the other wives did. This title made it so only the children Yesugei had with Hoelun would be heirs to Yesugei's position. Yesugei had two other sons from a previous marriage, but he had four more, one of which being Temujin, with his new captive wife.

Temujin was the second son born from Yesugei and Hoelun. He was born in 1162 and had one older brother, Hasar, and two younger brothers, Hachiun and Temuge. His older half brothers, Belgutei and Behter, were also a part of Temujin's childhood.

Temujin was born with a fighting spirit in his genes, being descended from some of the country's greatest warlords. It may be nothing more than ancient fable, but it is said that Temujin was born clutching onto a blood clot with his fist. This was meant as a sign that he would grow up to one day be a great leader, a prophecy that did indeed fulfill itself.

Ancestry and lineage was an incredibly important aspect of Mongolian social identity at this time, and scrupulous records were kept on family history. This meant that, by reputation alone, Temujin was born with more power than your average child born into a nomadic tribe. Even his name came with its own undeniable power. It is a name derived from two different Mongolian words. The first is temur, meaning "of iron," and the second is jin which is indicative of an agency or profession. So, roughly, Temujin translated to blacksmith; a noble, hardworking, and all important title of the time. It also was the name of a chieftain from a rivaling tribe, which Yesugei had captured right before his son's birth. The name brought with it a hardened sense of honor and respect, the likes of which Temujin would soon earn a reputation for in more than just name alone.

When it comes to the very early life of Temujin, not a whole lot is known. There was a fair amount of record keeping done at this time in history, but when you're talking about record keeping amongst disparate nomadic tribes, it is difficult to keep all of the details intact throughout history. But, while we might not know much of the specifics of the early days of Temujin, we do know the circumstances in which he grew up. Life on the road, living in nomadic conditions, was harsh to say the least. This was a region defined by war, and every sort of cutthroat tactic known to man could be expected in Mongolian conflict. Temujin likely grew up witnessing kidnappings, rape, and bloody conflict all around him. He was a witness of widespread tribal warfare, and had a front row seat to the vile revenge tactics these hotly contesting tribes employed on one another. Growing up in this environment obviously had an impact on the young Temujin. Before he was even old enough to comprehend the more complex political and societal strifes occurring before his eyes, the violence being used to get things done likely made an impression on his young mind.

It is around 1171 that we finally can begin to put concrete details to the life of Temujin. Mongolian society at the time was ruled, more than anything, by tradition. Power had shifted, been passed, and been established in similar ways throughout generations, and the value of namesake was crucial in keeping with Mongolian tradition. Children, much like women, were political commodities. Yesugei didn't have four children by Hoelun because he wanted a big, happy, loving family. He did this to secure his lineage, and spread his name by marrying off his sons to other tribes. This also aided in strengthening political ties between tribes. At the age of only nine years old Temujin found himself to be nothing more than a pawn in the political games of the region. An arranged marriage was set up for him, and he was to be married to Borte, a member of the Onggirat tribe, one of the various tribes comprising the Khamag Mongol confederation.

Temujin was brought to the Onggirats in 1171. He was nine at the time however, and Mongolian tradition stated that he could not marry until the age of twelve. He was to live in service to the head of the clan, Dai Setsen, for the next three years until he was old enough to marry Borte. These plans, however, were quickly squandered by unforeseen circumstances.

While Yesugei made his way back home, after dumping his son off with an allied tribe, he encountered another tribe which he did not hold the title of ally with. The Tatars were another of the five confederations comprising power in the Mongolian peninsula, and a Tatar general held captive by Yesugei is whom Temujin earned his name from. When Yesugei and the Tatars crossed paths, everything seemed friendly at first. Yesugei was invited to dine with the Tatars, with promises of an alliance on the horizon. This was not the case, as the Tatars had ulterior motives up their sleeves. They had poisoned the food which they offered to Yesugei, and he was given a swift, yet dreadful death at the hands of his enemies.

When news of his father's death reached Temujin, he realized he no longer had an obligation to Borte or the Onggirats, and he felt he was more needed with his family. Still just a child, Temujin returned home to take his father's position as head of the tribe. The confidence Temujin possessed as a ten year old was unprecedented, but the other members of the clan wanted nothing to do with him. They were not about to be ruled by a child. As far as they were concerned, with Yesugei dead any influence or control which he and his lineage retained on their tribe was dead with him. A family with which Yesugei had always had tensions with, the Tayichi'ud, usurped power over the Borjigin clan. Probably perceiving Temujin and his family as a threat to the clan's stability, as well as useless and weak additions to the tribe, the Tayichi'ud power banished Temujin and the rest of his family. On the next encampment move, Temujin, his mother, and the rest of his siblings were left behind to fend for themselves. Temujin now had a younger sister as well, Temulin, born just before Yesugei's death.

The family was banished to the woods, and left to depend totally on each other for survival. Hoelun and the children lived in awful poverty for years, barely scraping by on what scarce resources they could find in the woods and plains of Mongolia. Temujin and his brothers would hunt for small game like ox, marmots, or rabbits, while Hoelun would collect wild fruits and vegetables. Before he was even a teenager Temujin had experienced hardship unbeknownst to most of history's greatest leaders.

In 1172 Temujin's resilience was put to the ultimate test when he was forced to do something that would stick with him forever. As he and his family struggled through their abandonment, Behter, one of Temujin's two half-brothers, began to let his arrogance show. He was the oldest male in the family, and began to exercise that power. He made it a point that

Hoelun would have to marry him when he became an adult, so that he could assume his power over the tribe. He also made it a point that he would be exploiting his power, and would be unopposed in doing so, given that his siblings were so young and weak, or so he thought.

Temujin wasn't going to stand for this arrogance, and he especially wasn't going to allow the mistreatment of his mother. Women were a discredited proportion of Mongolian society, yet Hoelun did not let this affect her own sense of tenacity. She had an obligation to her children, and she kept this obligation close to her heart as she cared for Temujin and his siblings in their darkest hour of abandonment by their tribe. A fiery anger was building in Temujin towards his half-brother. His overzealous claim to the family name was pompous and obnoxious, but also just false, as Temujin and his full brothers were the true heirs of the late Yesugei, being that Hoelun was Yesugei's chief wife. This resentment towards Behter culminated during a hunting trip one day. Temujin, Behter, and Temujin's full brother Hasar, were out hunting one day, when Behter's arrogance became too much for Temujin and his brother to stomach. They turned their weapons on Behter, and at only ten years old Temujin struck down his own half-brother, and dealt him the killing blow.

Despite not being the oldest of the brothers, Temujin's actions solidified him as head of the family. It was clear that he was going to keep the family safe, and could lead them to safety and remove them from these terrible circumstances.

Over the next few years Temujin and his family wandered around Mongolia as a family of nomads, constantly scavenging for food day in and day out. Over time their stockpile became greater, and they became a small band capable of fending for themselves. Temujin displayed unprecedented charisma for his age, and could persuade his way out of harrowing situations, and always find a way to come out on top. The family over time managed to secure horses for themselves, as well as supporters who would travel with them for a trade of food, shelter, or security. Temujin found great loyalty in all who chose to be at his side, and at a young age he was already building strength and support around him.

Displays of Temujin's persuasiveness almost sound like tales of legend, yet they paint a very accurate picture of the kind of influence this great figure possessed. There was an incident shortly after the family had secured nine horses for themselves, where eight of those nine steeds were stolen by a band of thieves. Temujin refused to let these thieves enjoy their prize, and he set off in hot pursuit. Along the way he came across a stranger named Bo'orchu. Bo'orchu was busy milking his cow when Temujin rode up on his horse to ask the stranger if he had seen the stolen horses. Bo'orchu must have been completely enamored by the prowess of this young man bravely pursuing a gang of violent marauders just for his horses. His admiration compelled him to abandon his current duties, and instead equip Temujin with a fresh horse, and ride out with him to pursue the thieves. Their pursuit culminated in a success, the horses were stolen back, and Temujin was able to return them to his family. He returned to them with the eight horses, as well as Bo'orchu who, rather than accept a reward for his service, had sworn allegiance to Temujin as a nokor, meaning free companion. He clearly saw the makings of incredible things in the eyes of Temujin, as he had abandoned his own family to live and die in servitude to Temujin and his family. Bo'orchu's loyalty would not waver, and he would eventually serve as a general under Temujin, after he came to be known as Genghis Khan.

Temujin's charisma won him loyal friends and close companions, but it also saved his life a time or two. Sometime in 1177, when Temujin was only fifteen, the Tayich'ud family, old rivals of Temujin's father, raided their encampment and captured Temujin. This was done for the gain of resources, obviously, but it was also a chance to humiliate Temujin and his namesake. The Tayich'ud could have easily killed Temujin on the spot, but instead they imprisoned him, and fashioned him with a wooden cangue, a contraption more commonly known in the Western world as stocks. It was a degrading way to be imprisoned, but Temujin knew he was going to use this cockiness against his captors, and only had to wait for a matter of nights before he could do so.

One evening saw the clan distracted with festivities, likely celebrating some recent victory, or perhaps continuing to celebrate their most valuable prisoner. Regardless, the proceedings of the evening left Temujin poorly guarded. Only a single sentry stood in between Temujin and his escape, and so, using the weight of his cangue, he threw himself at the sentry, knocking him to the ground. This bought Temujin the time he needed to flee. His escape became known quickly, obviously, and a search initiated that lasted all night long. Temujin was almost caught when he was seen by one of the Tayich'ud. There was no way to tell what Temujin said or did to this guard to convince him to help him in his escape, rather than turn him in, but that's just what happened. Temujin and his new companion managed to escape the Tayich'ud, and that companion would later serve as a general under Genghis Khan. The Khan was not someone who forgot a face, or its loyalty, and his rule was characterized by rewarding these kinds of actions.

In a few short years of growth, Temujin had earned himself a reputation greater than that of most men double, even triple his age at the time. This reputation spread like wildfire, and it allowed Temujin and his family to regain their prominence amongst the Borgjin clan. Temujin was merely a teenager, but already he was becoming familiar with the feeling of power over both people and territory. He was now faced with political and traditional obligations in order to preserve the integrity of his tribe, and its place within the confederation. Temujin was coming of an age where he could see the power which he could attain if he played his cards right, and so he let his games begin.

Temujin knew he obviously needed as many allies as possible if he was going to begin changing the landscape and writing his own chapter of history. As was so very common with Mongolian tradition, marriage was the best way for him to secure at least one tribe's loyalty. He decided to return to the Onggirat tribe and marry Borte. The marriage occurred when Temujin was still only sixteen, but shortly afterwards, Borte was kidnapped by the Merkits, who themselves already possessed a lot of resentment for Temujin's bloodline. Temujin's own mother was originally a part of this tribal coalition before she was kidnapped by Yesugei, and this wasn't a fact the Merkits hadn't forgotten. They were horribly cruel to Borte, and Temujin knew he was going to rescue her and make her captives pay.

This wasn't something Temujin was going to be able to do alone, though. Lucky for him, between his bloodline and his own charming personality, he had resources available to him. Temujin first sought help from Toghrul, an old ally of his father's. Toghrul was the Khan of Keraites, another of the five confederations of the area. He was known to those at the time as Toghrul, but in 1197 would be granted the Chinese moniker of Wang Khan, bestowed to him by the Jurchen controlled Jin dynasty. Toghrul and Temujin's father had been integral players in establishing relations between the Mongol confederations. Their own personal friendship was very strong, and they had even established an anda between them. Anda's were sworn allies enacting a strong bond, a kind of blood brother relationship that was incredibly valued in Mongolian culture. Toghrul respected this title, and swore to support the bloodline of Yesugei. Thus, he equipped Temujin with an army of 20,000 soldiers.

Temujin sought help from another individual he was sure would come to his aid. This was Jamukha, a childhood friend of Temujin's. The two had grown up together, sharing childhood dreams of conquest and power. Their shared interests created a strong bond between the two, and they would also come to share the title of blood brothers between them. Of course, as they both grew older their desires for power sent them in opposite directions. Temujin was still on his course to holding an impressive title, but Jamukha had already found his own rise. He had risen to become Khan of the Jadaran tribe, and obviously felt the bloodlust driving his desire for conquest. He was reluctant to join Temujin at first, preoccupied with his own endeavors, and likely feeling a bit threatened by the fire in Temujin's eyes. With the help and persuasion of Toghrul, Jamukha was convinced to join forces with Temujin and help lead their cumulative army into battle with the Merkits. He might not have known it at the time, but as Temujin headed north to fight the Merkits and reclaim his captured wife, he was initiating the greatest period of change the Mongolian territories, including most of China and Central Asia, would ever know.

Chapter 14: Mongolia: A Rich History

Temujin, on his way to becoming Genghis Khan, was going to change the political, economic, and geographical landscape of his home territory. But, to fully understand the implications of what Temujin had set out to accomplish by initiating his first attack against a neighboring Mongol tribe, we must understand the history of this tumultuous region which brought it to where it was before 1206, the year Temujin would take his Khan title.

The geographical size and borders of what can be considered Mongolia was in a very liquid state for most of its history. Over the years power had shifted between tribal states and confederations, and the area can be constantly defined by warfare, whether Mongolia was trying to expand, or if it was trying to defend from Chinese invaders. It was not a region established with major cities and significant fortifications. Instead, Mongolia's ancient and medieval history is defined by nomads. The nomadic lifestyle was the only way of life at this time. This was common for the Central Asia reason, but due to geographic limitations, the nomadic lifestyle of Mongolia was different.

Mongolia is a uniquely situated region surrounded by harsh lands completely unsuitable for nomadic living. The region stretches out over the plains beneath the Altai Mountains, with rich rivers flowing through them. The river basins in the region made this area one of the most fertile lands in the world, and an excellent place to settle. Nomads relied on plentiful resources of wild fruits, veggies, and wildlife.

The geographic landscape essentially forced populations to inhabit this area, as opposed to the surrounding areas. To the North of the region was the frozen wasteland of Siberia, a place too deathly cold to even consider living and travelling with nothing more than tents and yurts. To the east was the growing

Chinese power, as well as the Indian Ocean. Migration south was not an option either, as the Gobi desert stretched for thousands of miles, making it deathly hot, and equally as uninhabitable as its freezing counterpart in the north. Then of course the Western front was marked by the Altai Mountains, and with such fertile plains at their disposal, living as a nomad in the mountains seemed counterproductive.

These geographical limitations essentially cut off Mongolia from the rest of the world. The majority of its major conflicts before Genghis Khan were with China, as their growing empirical power had the desire to be unstoppable at the time, and Mongolia seemed ripe for the taking. Much of ancient Mongolian history is defined by the power struggle between Mongolia and China.

It was in the third century BC that the first ruling establishment was put into power over the region. The Xiongnu state helped create a sense of shared identity and unity in the

Mongolian region, and a national desire for expansion was an enticing idea put into the heads of the tribal leaders. The Xiongnu were the very first people to invade China, and their arrival marked the first significant and consequential emergence of nomadic power in the region. The invasion was repelled, but caused enough of a stir for China to begin building their own fortifications to keep any future invaders, of which there would be plenty, out of their territory. These fortifications were all connected to one another to create a mighty 2,300 kilometer wall, otherwise known as the Great Wall of China.

The very first statehood established in Mongolia made a solid point that they were not part of the Chinese empire, and would exist as their own free region, a power on their own which was totally independent of China. This is one mindset that would remain consistent through pretty much the entirety of Mongolian history, long before and after the great Genghis Khan. The Chinese refuted these claims to power, and continued to wage war against the Mongolians all throughout their ancient history.

The Xiongnu ushered in a new era, bringing BC to AD, but the turn of the century saw their power begin to greatly diminish. By 48 AD the empire was split into norther and southern Xiongnu establishments, both of which left the Mongolian region to seek other prospects. The country was left vacant, and it wasn't long before another statehood had established dominance in the region.

In 93 AD the Xianbei took the place of the Xiongnu. They were up against the Han Dynasty of China, which was filled with national pride, and a desire to continue their campaigns against their nomadic neighbors. The Xianbei continued to fight off their attacks, while also extending their power to the West. The Xianbei marked a period of major growth for Mongolia, as they continued to cause unrest and dissention at the Chinese borders. As the Han Dynasty began to crumble, the Xianbei were able to exploit the internal strife and deterioration of the empire to grab a hold of more power than Mongolia had yet to know.

It was during the Xianbei rule that a faction of nomadic tribes broke off to the north, and established the Tuoba Wei. This clan gave way to the Rouran state, or Rouran Khaganate, which expanded even further north, gaining control of Eastern European territories. The Rouran ruling class was malicious, and massively subjugated the Altai Turkics. They enjoyed growing power to the West, while at the same time China had stopped persisting as such a threat.

It wasn't long before a new threat arose, and it came from what should have been an obvious place. In 552 the Turks revolted against the Rouran Khaganate and earned their own rule over the region, establishing the Turkic Khaganate that same year. Three years later they finished off the Rourans and assumed total dominance of the once Rouran state. It was perfect timing, too, because the Chinese empire was weaker than ever. They surrendered to the Turkic power without a fight.

The Turkic Khaganate remained in existence for nearly two hundred years, subjugating many Chinese populations, and in turn being subjugated by many as well. The power struggle was in full swing at this time, with the Chinese fighting valiantly for their sovereignty. Eventually, the Turkick Khaganate was split into Eastern and Western Turkic Khaganates, and their power quickly disseminated. The final blows were dealt in the seventh century, when the Western Turkics failed in an assault on Chang'an, the capital of China. They were turned away, utterly defeated. The Eastern Turkics continued to fight off subjugation and invasion by the Chinese, but were eventually defeated by a different enemy. The Uyghurs were a subjugated clan to the West that had known great turmoil in the Turkic invasions. In

745 they had had enough, and revolted to establish the Uyghur Khaganate.

Ironically, the takeover of the Uyghur Khaganate marked one of the first peaceful periods of Mongolian history. Trade routes were established between Mongolia and China, and relative prosperity was known across the land. When the Tang Dynasty took power over China, however, they held onto that resentment towards their neighbors to the West. Not wanting to risk dissention, they decided not to directly attack the region themselves. Instead, they encouraged others to do their biddings for them. In secret they convinced the Yenisei Kirghiz and the Karluks, two regions that the influence of Chinese politics and society still had a grip on, to invade the Uyghur Khaganate. An all out invasion by the Kirghiz took place in 840, and the Uyghur were utterly defeated, scattered across the Mongolian plains. Ironically, the Kirghiz had no interest in the region they had just conquered. They were established much further to the West, and control over

Mongolia was not in their intentions. Rather, it keeping good relations with the growing power of China that was in their best interest. Thus, the Mongolian region was left relatively empty, with dispersed nomadic tribes living in solidarity and having no influence over global society for the next sixty years or so.

The region knew no sort of statehood until a new leader, Ambagyan, rose up in 907 to establish the Khitan Liao Dynasty. The Liao Dynasty laid claim to most of the Mongolian region, assimilating the scattered peoples left over from the Uyghur Khaganate. This incredibly influential statehood quickly began posing another major threat to China. It grew rapidly, eventually controlling most of Northern China, at least everything north of the Yellow River. They were the first established power in the region to contest the idea of living the nomad life. They actually built cities which they could use as representations of their technical power, and innovative prowess, two things that helped show dominion and might over their subjects.

The Khitan state was, for all intents and purposes, a very successful one, bringing the country forward on a societal level. The Khitan people created their own alphabet, and printing technology also came to fruition in the area thanks to Khitan influence. Peace was known in the area once again until the Song Dynasty rose to power in China, and began to threaten the integrity of the Mongolian state. They did not have the capabilities to defeat the rapidly growing power of the Liao Dynasty, so they called upon the Jurchen, a Tungusic race of people, for assistance in their conquests. The coalition formed between the two powers waged a seven year war on The Liao Dynasty, which unsurprisingly tore the region to shreds.

By 1122 the Liao dynasty had denigrated into a vassal state, and their hold on the region was gone. It had been handed over to the Jurchen, whose leader declared himself the founder of this new era for China in the region. It was with the fall of the Liao dynasty that the Jin dynasty was born, and it came into the world fueled by bloodlust. The Jin wasted no time in spreading their conquests further, dominating the neighboring region of Goryeo, which is where Korea stands today. They even turned against the power which had called upon them in the first place, invading the Song dynasty in order to incite a whole cavalcade of ragged conflict in China. The Jin dynasty waited patiently for the dust to settle so they could lay claim to China, and the wait was worth it. The Jin dynasty would go on to become the ruling class of China for over 100 years, and they would not be challenged again until, you guessed it, Genghis Khan decided their influence needed to come to an end.

The Liao Dynasty marked the last time Mongolia was united under one statehood until Genghis Khan changed everything for the region. Internal struggle kept the country from going anywhere for the next few decades. Warring tribes kept up a consistent bout of anti-progress in the region, and the neighboring confederations trying to inject their own power and influence didn't help either. The beginning of Mongolia's medieval period was a rocky one to say the least. Tribes fended for themselves, and prosperity was nowhere to be found amidst these disparate plains.

The first semblance of a statehood began to reemerge early on in the 12th century. Warring tribes began consolidating, and putting their resources together to become a more unified power capable of fending off the always growing power of China, where the Jin dynasty retained gripping control. By about the halfway point of the century the Mongolian plateau was compromised of five major Mongolic tribal confederations, each with their own agendas, allegiances, and spheres of influence. Perhaps the strongest of these was the Khamag Mongol Khanate, placed in one of the most fertile regions of Mongolia, hidden away in the Khentii mountains at the base of the rivers Onon, Tuul, and Kherlen. This is the confederation of which Temujin was born into, and the one which his lineage had very strong ties to. It was Temujin's great grandfather, Khabul Khan, who became the first Khan of the Khamag Mongols, and it was he who would establish them as a legitimate power in the region.

The Jin obviously felt threatened by any amassment of power occurring in Mongolia, and so they sent an army to stomp out this growing threat, but Khabul Khan successfully repelled them, letting it be known that the Khamag Mongol Confederacy was a force to be reckoned with. Of course, they had other enemies to reconcile with as well.

One of the biggest adversaries of the Khamag Mongol confederacy was a rival confederacy known as the Tatars. The Tatars were a confederation neighboring Khamag Mongol to the East, and sharing a border with China. Before they fell, the Liao dynasty had enacted dominance over the Tatars. Thanks to the Jin invasion, the Tatars were freed from Mongolian subjugation, but this came with an obligation. There was a lot of pressure on the Tatars to throw their allegiance behind the Jin dynasty and, not wanting to face the consequences of denouncing their "saviors," their utmost support was given to their Chinese neighbors.

This period saw a lot of fighting between the Khamag Mongol and the Tatars, and the conflict would last up to Temujin's birth and beyond. When Khabul Khan stepped down from his Khanate duties, he was proceeded by Ambaghai Khan, who wanted to smooth relations with the Tatars. He tried to create an alliance by giving the Tatars his daughter as a bride. This peace seeking gesture was not reciprocated, unfortunately. Ambaghai was captured upon his arrival to the Tatar encampment, and the Tatars handed him straight over to their Jin allies. Upon receiving their prisoner, the Jin made their stance on the Khamag Mongol very clear. Ambaghai was swiftly executed, and then nailed to a wooden donkey for humiliation, and to send a violent message to their opposing forces on the Mongolian plateau.

It was Khabul Khan's son, Hotula Khan, who was elected to succeed Ambaghai and carry on the might of the Khamag Mongol, which refused to bend to the will of opposing forces, especially opposing Chinese forces. Hotula Khan led many an expedition against the Tatars, engaging in a total of thirteen battles with the confederation. The Tatars though, with the backing of the Jin power, were unable to be defeated completely, and retained their power in the East. In the last of these Khamag/Tatar engagements, Hotula Khan was killed, and the Khamag Mongol confederation was left without a Khan. Internal struggles within the confederation halted any political progress, and a new Khan was not elected. Instead, Yesugei, Temujin's father, came on as a supervisor and representative of the confederacy, along with the heads of the other major Khamag Mongol tribes. In 1171 the Tatars revealed that their grudge was still not over when the poisoned and killed Yesugei. This may have been a strategic move for them at the time, but it certainly painted a huge target on their backs for when Temujin decided he was ready to take his revenge and begin his conquests of Mongolia.

.

Three other confederations existed by the time Temujin was born, yet didn't know quite the power that the Khamag Mongols or the Tatars knew. The first was the Keraite Khanate. The Keraites were a Turco-Mongol tribal confederation who retained a tight grip on their power in Southern Mongolia. They were defined by a deeply loyal army with soldiers who valiantly and unwaveringly served the Khan, and the Khan alone. The Keraites were originally part of the Zubu confederacy, which they comprised the ruling class of. The Zubu confederacy had been a major adversary of the Liao dynasty, and the two had fought tirelessly for control of

Mongolia. When the Liao dynasty was forced out by the Jin, the Zubu consolidated to the Keraites, and they reestablished themselves in southern Mongolia. Around the time of Temujin's birth is when the young Toghrul, son of Kurchakus Buyruk Khan, claimed the throne of the Keraites and became Toghrul Khan. His claim was legitimate, as his grandfather, Markus Buyruk Khan, had led the Keraites against the Liao dynasty at the turn of the 12th century. Toghrul became a close ally with the Khamag Mongol confederacy, becoming blood brothers with the late Yesugei.

Another of the five confederacies of the time were the Naimans. This small tribe began their growth in the heart of Mongolia, but had since moved further West. Another confederacy of Turkic origin, the Naimans used this lineage to establish relative peace with other Khanates of the area, such as the Khitan Khanate, also known as Qara Khitai. The Naimans led an existence under the radar, serving powers far greater than theirs to ensure some sort of peace, or at least prolonged survival for their heritage. They proved to be a resilient people who, even after the dissemination of Mongolian confederacies and tribes, continued to have a presence all over the region.

The last of the five confederacies was the Merkit, the confederation that had foolishly kidnapped Temujin's wife, and who would be the first victims of Temujin's unstoppable warfare. The Merkits were comprised of three tribes, otherwise known as the Three Merkits. These were the Uduyid Merkits, who inhabited the lower regions of the Orkhon River, the Uvas Merkits, who lived in between the Orkhon and Selenge Rivers, and the Khaad Merkits, who called the Selenge River bank home. The Merkits operated separately from any of the other powers in the region, but clearly were defined by a grudge against the Khamag Mongols. This certainly had to do with the fact that Yesugei had stolen Hoelun, his wife and Temujin's mother, from their tribe, never to return her.

Chapter 15: Uniting Mongolia

To say that the political stability of Mongolia was shaky during Temujin's adolescence would be an understatement. He grew up surrounded by political turmoil, and spent his childhood learning what did and didn't work in a military campaign. He grew up dangerously smart, and now the time had finally come for him to use his insight directly, and lead a charge that would establish him as a dominant force to be reckoned with, along with displaying the punishments that should be expected for crossing him.

The Merkits knew that Temujin would be coming for Borte, but what they didn't know is the size of the army which he had managed to put behind him. Between the forces of himself, Toghrul, and Jamukha, Temujin was leading a viciously destructive army; one that would be incredibly dangerous to get in the way of.

Temujin and his allies handily defeated the Merkits. They managed to route them, and Temujin was able to practice his strategy of not leaving a single enemy force behind him in his wake. He came in swiftly and destructively, never giving the Merkits a chance for survival. Temujin looked for his conquests to be absolute, and made sure to leave none alive that had the will, the tenacity, or the downright stupidity to oppose him. Merkit nobility were slaughtered, while the common population was assimilated under the Mongolian power which Temujin represented. This would be a very common practice for Temujin, and it was incredibly useful in growing his army, as well as giving him a favorable view in the eyes of the general public. He sought to be more of a liberator for the common people, and a dangerously murderous opposition to the royal class individuals, at least in Mongolia.

Temujin's campaign against the Merkits couldn't have been more successful. He had defeated the first of Khamag Mongol's surrounding enemies, and had also reclaimed his wife. When he and Borte were reunited it was a joyous occasion defined by actual love. Nine months after her rescue Borte had her first child, Jochi. It was assumed that Jochi was the son of Borte and Temujin, but there is no certainty on this. Borte, during her captivity, was likely given away as a wife to one of the Merkit chieftains, or someone in their nobility. Given the timing of Jochi's birth, this will remain as one of history's unsolved mysteries.

Even though Temujin and Jamukha had enjoyed a great victory together, jealously and pettiness would begin to drive their friendship apart. Their childhood bond was shaken by Temujin's prolific military capabilities. Jamukha saw Temujin as a threat to his own want for power, and this is something he openly expressed. The friendship between the two men was on the rocks as they returned from Merkit, and it was completely shattered once they both began pursuing their own rises to power. It became increasingly obvious that their pride wouldn't allow them to reconcile, and only one of them could emerge victorious

in retaining power over the growing Mongol state. It wasn't long before they had gone incredibly far away from their friendship, and could now be considered adversaries.

Temujin and Jamukha had drastically different viewpoints on how Mongolia should be governed, and this was likely one of the many reasons their rift developed as they both simultaneously began eyeing power. Jamukha was the traditionalist out of the two men. He believed in the ancient Mongolian power structure, which gave power to a noble class of elitists. These elitists had no merits but their name. Lineage and family name was the basis for the appropriation of power, and Temujin saw this as an incredibly unfit way to divide strength. He believed those with power should possess the personal attributes which make them deserving of that power. He assigned positions based on the talent of the individual, and their loyalty to him. Temujin felt this created a far more dedicated powerhouse to surround himself with. The aristocracy method alienates all of the lower class populations, which Temujin relied on for his growth in power and popularity. His meritocratic policies engaged a much broader collection of supporters, and his popularity amongst the masses posed a major threat to Jamukha.

As it became more and more obvious that Temujin was vying for ultimate power over Mongolia, Jamukha became increasingly worried that he would accomplish this. He had obviously shown his unbridled military might in his campaign against the Merkits, and was seen as a friend of the people, something which the shady and enigmatic Jamukha did not have working in his favor. Even prophecy was acting on behalf of Temujin. A shaman named Kokochu proclaimed that the Eternal Blue Sky, essentially the prevailing God of Mongolia's shamanistic religion, had "set aside the world for Temujin." He was going to barrel towards that power which he knew he could attain, and would be unopposed in doing so if Jamukha didn't step in.

In 1186 the final straw broke Jamukha, and prompted him to take action. This was the year that Temujin was elected Khan of the Khamag Mongol confederation. He had been given the keys to a massive power grab of the entire region, and this worried Jamukha greatly. He acted quickly, and amassed an army containing 30,000 soldiers who had agreed to support his rise to power. Temujin was taken off guard by this sudden hostility from a man he was once able to call friend, and was not prepared in the slightest to deal with an opposing force of this magnitude. Temujin didn't expect his next adversary to come from within, and this was his downfall. He suffered a grave defeat at the Battle of Dalan Balzhut in the year 1187 , and was subsequently exiled by Jamukha, who was now invigorated with ruthless fire.

Jamukha was particularly harsh in his ousting of Temujin, which would not work in his favor in the long run. He took a number of captives in his victory, and selected 70 of these captives to be boiled alive in a cauldron. It was a grotesque and unnecessary act that most certainly turned people against Jamukha. He had every intention to rule by fear, using his power to quell his own insecurities and live the ruling lifestyle he wished to live, which was one that kept himself safe before anyone else. This only drew sympathy for the exiled Temujin, and Jamukha would never know the popularity which he likely longed for.

Temujin had lost his grip on the Khamag Mongols, but this wouldn't stop him from consolidating his forces and looking for other ways to gain power. Toghrul was exiled along with him, so he still had a valuable ally at his side. There exists a ten year period of Temujin's life, stretching between 1187 and 1197, that has scarce historical record verifying anything that happened in this time.

It is likely that Temujin was amassing his forces, making sure to lie low during the growing might of Jamukha. Jamukha had been a setback in his plans for taking total control over the Mongol regions, but he knew there were other ways to go about achieving what he set out to do.

This period of time was likely about reputation for Temujin. He was technically nothing more than a low ranking chieftain after his exile, and could easily paint himself to be of no concern to other tribes. He kept his allegiance with Toghrul strong as the two built up their forces and planned their next move into the Mongolian confederations. Temujin had obviously been eyeing the Tatars for a while now. They held strategically important land to the West, and were also the murderers of his father. He wanted to inflict revenge, more than anything, on these people. His opportunity to do so came in 1197.

Temujin had made himself seem totally non-threatening to the Chinese Jin dynasty, all for the purpose of using their prowess for his next move. Temujin and his Mongol forces, along with Toghrul and his Keraite army formed an alliance with the Jin in order to launch a massive assault on the Tatars. Temujin might not have been the primary leader in this attack, but he used his allied resources wisely, and was part of a huge victory over the Tatars. The confederation was all but wiped out, with very few surviving populations being scattered across the region. The Jin showed their great admiration for Temujin and Toghrul by reinstating their power in the region. Toghrul was even bestowed with the highly respected title of Wang Khan. Temujin and Toghrul were now back in a strengthened position to continue their plight of the Mongol confederations. At least for now, they perceived no threat from China, as the Jin obviously didn't see the two of them as much of a substantial force. They could focus all of their attention on their own region, now, and fight back against what the tyrannical Jamukha was trying to do with his harsh rule. In 1201 he had been appointed as Gur Khan, a title which translates to universal ruler most commonly used by the Qara Khitai.

At this point, there were only two confederations which still posed a threat to the power of Temujin and Toghrul, and these were the Merkits to the north and the Naimans to the west. In a series of short yet bloody campaigns, the Merkits were easily defeated, and their namesake was completely scattered. The vast majority of Merkit populations and culture was absorbed by what was coming to be known as Temujin's Mongol confederation. The rest sided with the Naimans.

Jamukha's power had been reduced to nothing more than his control over the Naiman populations, and this was the last great opposition to Temujin within Mongolia. Before he led his campaign into Naiman territory, though, a deteriorating friendship delayed his progress.

There were hardly any signs of this estrangement, but around 1201 Toghrul decided he could not let Temujin continue his unabashed power trip. Toghrul didn't come to this conclusion entirely on his own, but rather was influenced by his son, Senggum. Senggum saw Temujin as the all powerful warlord he would become, and was mighty jealous of how easily Temujin was amassing this power. He was likely frustrated, seeing as his father was aiding Temujin in this great battle for domination, but seeing little reward of his own. Given their rich history, Toghrul had always considered himself an unwavering ally of Temujin and his namesake, and Senggum saw issue with this blind faith. Toghrul was pulled violently in opposing directions, but ultimately had to leave his loyalty with his son. He listened closely to all that Senggum was putting in his ear, leading him to become adversarial towards Temujin, refusing to play the game of political maneuvers that Temujin needed his help with.

Toghrul illustrated this break in friendship concisely when he allowed Senggum to go forward with a plan to assassinate Temujin. Lucky for Temujin, he caught wind of Senggum's plans, and put a quick end to them. Senggum's followers were killed, while Senggum managed to escape, eventually finding refuge with the Xi-Xia to the south. It was now more apparent than ever that the friendship between Toghrul and Temujin had come to an end.

Yet, just in case the message wasn't clear enough, Toghrul let one more action drive home the split in their relationship. Temujin needed a wife for his eldest son, Jochi, and wanted it to be a marriage that solidified an important political partnership. In a last attempt to reconcile their friendship, he requested that Toghrul marry his daughter to Jochi. Toghrul adamantly refused, an act that could be perceived as treasonous in Mongolian culture. The rift was more apparent than ever, and now would begin to take its toll on not just the two men as individuals, but on the world.

Now that they were staunch adversaries, Toghrul sought a way to defeat Temujin, and he found his best option was to seek a former enemy by the name of Jamukha. Toghrul and Jamukha formed a hesitant partnership, and consolidated their forces with the Keraites. Temujin's victories had already given him the reputation he needed to lead any campaign he put his mind to, and as soon as he set out on his campaign to end the alliance between Toghrul and Jamukha, dissention began. Jamukha only knew power by force, and had none of the benevolence of Temujin that had earned him such loyal soldiers. An army without fighting spirit was one that was absolutely terrified by the might of Temujin. Uninspired by the leadership of Jamukha, and the flakiness of Toghrul, many of their allies abandoned them before Temujin and his forces even showed up. As Jamukha's army dwindled, Temujin's only grew. Toghrul, likely aware of his mistake, harshly butted heads with his supposed ally, and their leadership over what army they were left with was practically non-existent. Jamukha's presence led to the crumbling of the Keraite infrastructure long before Temujin's forces would show up. The two arrogant leaders, drowned in their own hubris, didn't stand a chance when Temujin did arrive.

Temujin's campaign against the Keraites in 1203 was another swift and destructive one. It scattered populations and absorbed even more soldiers and civilians. Jamukha managed to flee the fighting, and made his way to Naiman, the last confederacy that could pose as any semblance of safety for him and anyone else who opposed Temujin's rapid rise to power. Toghrul was not so lucky. He managed to flee as well, but when he met up with Naiman soldiers during his escape, they mistook him for a member of the enemy army, and killed him on sight. Just like that, Toghrul, a name that had so much weight and prowess behind it in the early days of the Mongolian confederations, was now dead, due to an embarrassing defeat in an ill-advised, unprepared campaign. Temujin proved himself to be more resilient than any military leader at the time, and showed the world that any who opposed him did so foolishly.

Despite all of the defeats, Jamukha was still not prepared to concede to Temujin. A man he had once valued as a friend and insightful colleague, he was now vowing to oppose till his dying breath. He assumed power in Naiman, and continued to uphold his promise of rejecting Temujin's growing influence over the Mongolian plateau. Temujin was ready to eliminate this issue for good, and formed a coalition of tribes aiming to bring Jamukha to his knees. Jamukha had the strength of his own coalition, the one that elected him Gur Khan in 1201, and was ready to fight against him. Temujin did not want to kill his childhood friend, whose character he still valued, but he was ready to strip the man of every last bit of power he might possibly retain, so as to remove him as a threat once and for all.

It seems that Jamukha is the only person in the entire world at the time that failed to realize he didn't stand a chance against Temujin. He would hear no calls for peace, or even stalemate. He was convinced that Mongolian society could never move forward if both of the men remained alive. His thirst for victory over his former ally was sad, almost desperate, and his forces could see this fact plain as day. Before the campaign got underway, Jamukha was abandoned by a number of his generals, who switched sides to fight for the far more promising Temujin.

Temujin was likely trying to prompt a surrender, but Jamukha wasn't going to give him the satisfaction. He forced more fighting to occur, and a number of battles went underway that eventually led to Jamukha's defeat. Not a defeat on the battlefield, however. Fed up with his arrogant tactics which were sending hundreds of Naiman soldiers to their death, Jamukha's own men mutinied and turned him in to Temujin in 1206.

Temujin displayed clemency once again, and offered Jamukha his life. He had the men who turned in Jamukha killed, as he did not want disloyal men to be a part of his army. He surely hoped this would show Jamukha that he still valued their friendship, and was still willing to reconcile. It was Temujin's final attempt at bringing Jamukha back to his side, but Jamukha once again refused. He told Temujin that there could be only one sun in the sky, affirming Jamukha's stance that there would never be peace or unity amongst the Mongol confederations with both of them still standing. He refused to stand at Temujin's side, and instead requested an honorable death. It was customary that a noble death was one that involved no bloodshed, and rather involved the breaking of one's back. And so, Temujin had his own childhood friend, a close companion who had devolved into a power hungry madman who boiled his enemies alive in cauldrons, put to a noble death, and had his back broken. Jamukha may have died full of resentment towards Temujin, but Temujin respected Jamukha until his dying breath. He even buried Jamukha with the golden belt he had given to him when their blood brother bond was forged. And so ended a tragic saga of two estranged friends.

With this death, Temujin finally found himself unopposed in Mongolia. The last of the Naimans were dealt with swiftly, and any Merkit opposition that had joined forces with them was handled in the same sweep. Temujin was now the unopposed conqueror of the Mongolian steppe, and he had officially established his own Mongol confederation which united all tribes under one unifying association. 1206 would be the last year Temujin answered to that name. His name would now be defined by his title, and that title was of course the mightily ominous moniker of Genghis Khan.

Chapter 16: Mongolia Under Khan

1206 was THE vital turning point in Mongolian history and, in fact, world history. The structure of Mongolian politics was shattered. Tribes and clans were dispersed, and retained no individual power. They were now unified under one code, one ideal, and one ruler. The mass of land that had housed the Khamag Mongol, the Tatars, the Merkits, the Keraites, the Naimans, and various others, would now come to be known only as Mongolia, or the Mongol Empire.

That year, the noble families of the Mongolian tribes met at the kurultai, the council of Mongol chiefs which met to elect new Khans. Temujin was elected unanimously, given that he had more than proven himself worthy. It was the first time in medieval history that Mongolia had been unified. They were now a collective force which possessed the strength in numbers needed to expand, and they had the ruler they would need to make their mark on history. Temujin's military ability had been unmatched, and it was clear he was the only one of them worthy to lead the armies of the consolidated Mongolia into battle. Total power was given to Temujin, and the kurultai overwhelmingly elected him to be their new great Khan, and their universal ruler. They chose him and gave him that legendary title of Genghis Khan.

Genghis Khan sought to completely revolutionize this newly conformed empire he now had universal leadership over. Genghis wasn't only looking for immeasurable power for himself. He also sought peace and prosperity for the empire of Mongolia, and that could only be achieved with a ground-up restructuring of the entire Mongolian political system that had given tribes and clans dispersed power. The social and political hierarchy was a convoluted one, and Genghis in turn consolidated their power to himself, and made sure that he was the only presence which the Mongolian people answered to. He was the sole ruler of the steppe, and knew he could only retain this power if he was treated as such. With the prowess of his stature solidified, he could enact sweeping changes meant to benefit Mongolian people and society, and bring the empire to a more prosperous point of great influence on the world.

The seeds of this sole leadership structure had already been planted during Genghis' campaigns against his rival nomadic tribes. In each of his victories he absorbed the common people under his rule. Members of rival tribes would be guaranteed protection under Genghis' subjugation, and they would be appropriately integrated into his unified society. Genghis even had his mother adopt orphans left behind in his raids, and integrate them into the family.

Genghis pushed a belief on his people that loyalty to him would result in rewards for them, and disloyalty would be reciprocated appropriately. He was a fair conqueror who believed in redemption. Military leaders who opposed him, once defeated, would be given the chance to swear their allegiance to the Khan. Many of those who did were allowed to keep their military ranking, only now they served the Mongol Empire and Genghis Khan first and foremost.

Genghis' system of meritocracy completely went against Mongolian tradition, but Genghis was more focused on building an undyingly loyal support system beneath him, rather than adhere to ancient customs. His strategy was to put the most able bodied individuals in positions of power that they deserved due to their skillset or personality. Social status, heritage, and religion, were not factors in delegating duties, and this made for an incredibly diverse population under Genghis. He also underwent multiple restructurings of his army, so that all cultures were mixed together, and soldiers could be identified by their ranking and their ability, rather than their family history. These major shake-ups of Mongolian tradition marked the beginning of a new era for the country which would continue long after Genghis Khan's death. It was the beginning of Pax Mongolica.

Pax Mongolica translates to "Mongol Peace," and is in reference to Pax Romana, the era of relative peace that the Roman Empire enjoyed just after Emperor Augustus took over. Ironically, Pax Romana was defined by a lack of military expansionism which resulted in the Roman Empire getting back on its feet after the destruction of the Roman Republic. Pax Mongolica is defined by the peace that was spread through Genghis Khan's violent campaigns across the Western world. The idea was an ambition of Genghis' that he wanted to instate across his growing territory, and he would do so by any means necessary.

Before any expansion could take place, Genghis knew it was important that the current state of the Mongolian empire was a prosperous one, but one that was controlled within specific confines that would direct society towards peace. He divided lands and money in a far more fair and balanced manner with much more even distribution between nobles, which included the empresses, princesses, and meritorious servants. He also distributed fairly and evenly to his soldiers, whom he allowed to keep their war spoils.

Mongolia was now under a uniquely new unified rule, and Genghis sought to do away with ancient traditions which used to restrict the territory. He sought to unify his culturally diverse Mongolian population under one code of law, which could be applied universally. Genghis wrote these laws up himself, and called them the Yassa. The Yassa code of law was an intriguing one, given that its exact contents were actually kept secret. The separate provisions covered by the Yassa were decreed when necessary, with very few individuals having access to the whole comprehensive list of laws. This allowed the Yassa to be modified without a single sole knowing, meaning provisions could be altered or added when necessary for the benefit of Genghis. It was also the de facto law of the land. De facto roughly translates from Latin to "in fact." This meant that the laws were not officially beset by a higher power, but rather they were the universally accepted laws that existed in practice, rather than official documentation. The Yassa was likely written down in one comprehensive text stowed away by Genghis, but no complete list of the Yassa has ever been discovered.

The Yassa may have been put into practice in a shady manner, enforced only by the will of Genghis Khan and his followers, but the laws themselves did in fact have good intentions meant to keep peace and structure social hierarchy in a fair and appropriate way. The Yassa began to be compiled as a series of decrees applying directly to war and Genghis' warfare tactics. His rulings divided his army and created the effective restructuring of his men into groups of tens, hundreds, or thousands, led by trustworthy leaders who swore their loyalty to the Khan.

There were a variety of provisions in the Yassa which aimed to give structure to warfare, and they turned the Mongolian army into a highly respectable one. Soldiers were required to receive their battle equipment from no one other than their commanding officer, and they were personally in charge of keeping their equipment in good condition. Genghis was incredibly serious about his army being properly stocked and prepared, and their weapons and armor would be carefully examined before each campaign. Soldiers that did not take care of their equipment up to the proper standards, or lacked a piece of equipment entirely, were punished.

Soldiers were not allowed to begin a pillage of their enemy unless granted permission by their commanding general. However, once the general had given this permission, soldiers were allowed to keep whatever they pillaged. This was greatly effective in boosting morale, allowing these soldiers to walk away from campaigns with their own personal spoils of war. This provision maintained a happy army, but those who abused their privileges could face severe punishment. Negligence was an offense that could be punished by a severe beating, or even death. Sharing clothing or food with a prisoner of war, unless give permission by the captor, was punishable by death. It was also forbidden for armies to make any kind of peace with an enemy who had not yet submitted to the will of Genghis Khan and the Mongolian Empire.

Genghis developed a multitude of provisions in his Yassa that aimed to harden the loyalty around him, and keep the fires of this loyalty burning strong for his and future generations. One of the ways he did this was by disallowing any subject of the Mongolian Empire to be taken as a slave. Every man in the empire was required to give service, at least for a time, to the Empire. Service to the empire generally meant going to war for them, but those who didn't go off to battle were still required to serve in other capacities. This could have been any number of duties meant to serve and strengthen the army.

Some of the laws decreed by Genghis' Yassa seemed quite strange, yet still must have served some political, religious, or cultural interest for the Khan. For instance, the cutting of an animal's throat to use it for food was banned, and instead it was officiated that animals must be hung by their feet, their stomach's ripped open, and their heart squeezed until death. It also legitimized children born of concubines, meaning these children had entitlement to their father's inheritance, should the father allow it. This decree likely stems from the polygamist attitudes of Mongolian society. Genghis himself had a vast amount of wives in his lifetime, the exact number of which is unknown. Other somewhat strange provisions that likely stemmed from cultural history included the banning of bathing or washing clothes during a thunderstorm, or washing clothes before they were totally worn out. Additionally, subjects were not allowed to dip their hands into water to drink, but rather they were required to use a receptacle. The provisions also forbade individuals to reference each other with a title, and were instead required to acknowledge each other by their given name.

Throughout the Yassa the punishments are notably harsh, and the words, "put to death" can be frequently seen. Any divisiveness within the army was punishable by death, but a number of other practices also came with capital punishment. If you were to find a slave and failed to return that slave to his owner, you could be put to death. If you were found guilty of adultery you could be put to death. Liars, spies, and those that practiced witchcraft or sorcery were also placed under the death penalty. The death penalty seemed to be the most universal form of punishment that was applied to multiple levels of crimes, and discriminated against no one. Even high ranking generals could be put to death if they failed in their duties, or failed to show up when called upon by the Khan. Criminals who kidnapped or sexually assaulted women were given this ultimate punishment, but it was also something applied to liars, cheaters, thieves, and those who disrespected their elders. Even crimes as tame as urinating into water or ashes were punishable by death. The sweeping power of the death penalty shows us what a different and far more ruthless time in history this was. Sodomy was another action punishable by death, which likely means that homosexuality was perceived as a heinous crime.

We may be able to associate a lot of cruelty with the Yassa, but there was one hugely revolutionary aspect to the code which shows the positive progression Genghis hoped to achieve through it. The Yassa was the first code of law which displayed religious tolerance. No leader had ever given such blanket tolerance of such a thing, but Genghis Khan was unlike other leaders. He even gave tax exemptions to places of worship, a custom seen in modernized countries today like the United States. His wasn't complete tolerance, though, as it was still required that all subjects maintained their belief in one God, but that God could be worshiped in whatever way suited the individual. Genghis decreed no singular religion for Mongolia, and allowed subjects to practice essentially any religion they wished. All religions were required to be given respect, and the empire would display no preference towards any of them. Removing religion as one of the pillars of civilized society, and allowing a more or less free range of practice, was unprecedented.

Genghis himself was a tengrist, or one who practices Tengrianism. This ancient religion dominated most of the Central Asian region at the time. It combined principles of shamanism and animism, as well as the worship of ancestors. It was a religion that coincided well with Mongolian lifestyle. The nomadic life required a strong coalition between man, animal, and nature to survive harsh conditions and domesticate wild animals for use. The shamanistic beliefs gave power to the earth, wind, and sky, and animism perpetuated the integrity of animals, and gave way to the idea they each had souls that needed to be respected. This way of thinking had aided Genghis as he grew up Temujin, but as his scope of the world became bigger, his tolerance of the world's diversity became a defining characteristic of his. Genghis always remained curious about other ways of thinking and what they could offer him and society. He was open to learning all he could about various religions, and even consulted great religious leaders. Throughout his life Genghis met with Buddhist monks, Christian missionaries, and Muslims in the Middle East. He also met with Qiu Chuji, the most famous of the Seven True Daoists of the North to discuss life, death, and immortality.

The only religious groups that did seem to receive any sort of subjugation from Genghis were the Muslims and Jews, and this may have been because of some of Islam's practices towards animals and food which went directly against shamanism or animism.

For instance, Halal butchering, or the practice of slitting an animals throat, was banned, hence the section of the Yassa which gave far more specific instructions on how to slaughter animals for food. Genghis did take some particularly harsh actions against these groups, calling Muslims and Jews slaves, and forbidding the halal method of eating. Kosher eating was banned, and the Mongol diet was enforced upon these populations. Circumcision was also banned. For all that Genghis did for religious tolerance, he still had his downfalls, but his growing acceptance as he got older reflected a way of thinking quite progressive for the time.

Now, with the power of the Khan title strengthening his claims, Genghis Khan was ready to expand. Mongolia had enjoyed relatively the same sects of land for the entirety of their existence. Genghis now saw it as time to break past these borders which had been culturally, societally, and geographically imposed on them. He saw the Empire as just that, an Empire. Empires don't just retain control of their relatively small plot of land. They push their borders in all directions, looking to impose the will of their leader everywhere they conquer.

Genghis's ambitions were not born completely from a lust for conquest. Rather, he was fueled by the desire to expand Mongolia's prosperity, creating a unified population in Asia which was diverse in culture, religion, and heritage, but united under a common code of law, and extensive trade routes. Creating a more expansive trade network was going to be a major focus of Khan's during his expansion of the empire. He saw the necessity in having strong networks to trade goods, as the area they currently possessed offered little in the way of viable trading resources. The Silk Road cut through a significant portion of Mongolia, and Genghis made it an intention to expand control over areas the Silk Road also merged with, creating a unified economic network under his empire.

Even before the unification of the Mongol tribes, Genghis was accepting of foreign merchants, and had always been a supporter of international trade. Merchants were also a viable source of information which Genghis used to gather intelligence on his enemies. He saw economic interdependence as a majorly important aspect of society that was necessary for prosperity.

An interconnected society was a very important ideal to Genghis, and he made this clear early on in his takeover of Mongolia. Mongolia can actually be credited for the establishment of one of the earliest postal services in history, referred to in Mongolian history as the Yam. Genghis himself was responsible for one of the most significant expansions of this system, and used it more effectively than most of his predecessors. The Yam was an extensive route system that stretched across the country and was used by messengers to deliver important intel back and forth between cities. It was critical that information move quickly for Genghis, as his armies themselves already moved quickly. The Yam was essentially a series of relay stations, each around 200 kilometers apart, that messengers travelled back and forth from, in a type of relay chain that moved letters, supplies, or horses, from one station to the next. This, along with Genghis's network of spies which operated using the Yam, was one of his greatest assets.

One of the most peaceful times Mongolian history had ever known up to that point had been officially established, and Genghis Khan took primary credit for it. He had the unabashed and stalwart support of the people backing his desire to expand. His soldiers were valiant weapons of his that answered to the will of the Khan before anyone else. He had their undying loyalty, and knew this support made his army mightier than any that might oppose him. All of Mongolia now answered to him, and he was going to use this power for the good of the

Empire first and foremost. It was time to grow, time to enact dominance of Asia, taking revenge on all those nations and empires which tried to subjugate Mongolia in the past. The region had long standing grudges in every direction, and Genghis Khan sought to put an ultimatum on these grudges. How would he do that?

Complete and utter conquest, of course. With the unwavering support of the people behind him, along with one of the most massive armies history had ever seen, Genghis was ready to begin the most significant chapter of his life. He was ready for military conquest.